Study Guide and Personal Growth Exercises to Accompany

Psychology and Effective Behavior

L. N. Jewell

Prepared by
Sandra L. Dunn, M.S.
Western Kentucky University

Thomas P. Dunn, Ph.D.
Western Kentucky University

West Publishing Company
St. Paul   New York   Los Angeles   San Francisco

COPYRIGHT © 1989 by WEST PUBLISHING CO.
　　　　　　　50 W. Kellogg Boulevard
　　　　　　　P.O. Box 64526
　　　　　　　St. Paul, MN 55164-1003

All rights reserved
Printed in the United States of America
96 95 94 93 92 91 90 89   8 7 6 5 4 3 2 1 0
ISBN 0-314-52486-X

Contents

PART I: INTRODUCTION

Chapter 1   Introduction..1
Chapter 2   You and Your Environment: The Foundations of Behavior...13

PART II: YOU: A UNIQUE INDIVIDUAL

Chapter 3   Your Cognitive, Emotional and Moral Development.........25
Chapter 4   Personality: You as Others See You......................35
Chapter 5   The Self and Self-Concept: You as You See Yourself......47

PART III: YOUR WORLDS

Chapter 6   Your Social World: Attraction and Friendship............59
Chapter 7   Your Intimate World: Sex and Sexual Relationships.......75
Chapter 8   Your Special Relationships: Love and Marriage...........91
Chapter 9   The Worlds of Education and Work.......................109

PART IV: BASIC SKILLS FOR MORE EFFECTIVE BEHAVIOR

Chapter 10   Communication and Communicating........................123
Chapter 11   Decisions and Decision Making..........................141
Chapter 12   Stress and Stress Management...........................153

PART V: PROBLEMS THAT BLOCK EFFECTIVE BEHAVIOR

Chapter 13   Behavior Management Problems...........................171
Chapter 14   Relationship Problems..................................187
Chapter 15   Emotional and Psychological Problems...................205

PART VI: GETTING HELP

Chapter 16   Resources for More Effective Behavior..................221

PERSONAL GROWTH EXERCISES

Who Are You..9
The Scientific Method.......................................11
The Youth Culture...21
The Power of Personal and Social Constraints................23
Your Moral Development......................................33
Learning Processes..34
Do You See Yourself As Others See You?......................44
Your Personality..45
Your Own Needs Hierarchy....................................56
Self-Concept..57
Friendship..71
Self-Disclosure...72
Friendships...73
Your Sexuality..87
Sexual Stereotypes..89
Your Love Triangles..103
Are You Ready For Love?....................................104
Why Do You Fall In Love?...................................106
Choosing Your Occupation...................................119
Career Development...120
The Interview..121
Loaded Word Activity.......................................136
Reading Nonverbal..137
Lack of Communication......................................139
Methods of Communication...................................140
Your Decision Making Style.................................150
Where Do You Make Your Decisions...........................151
Your Reactions to Stress...................................163
The Effects of Stress......................................165

Shyness..166
Time Management Skills...168
Alcohol Abuse..183
Addictions...185
Reflective Listening...198
Communication in Marriage..200
Common Complaints in Marriage....................................203
Emotional and Psychological Problems.............................216
Worry..218
What Type of Therapy...233
Your Own Problems..235

To the Student...

This study guide was prepared to help you learn the materials in Jewell's <u>Psychology and Effective Behavior</u>, and to help you to apply what you have learned to your own present and future life circumstances.

Each chapter contains Learning Objectives, a Chapter Outline, and Review Questions which include: Matching; Fill-In, True-False, Multiple-Choice Questions; and a People You Should Know section. Each chapter also contains at least two Personal Growth Exercises. The answers to the Matching, Fill-In, True-False, and Multiple-Choice Questions may be found at the back of this guide. The Personal Growth Exercises will, of course, be different for every individual who completes them.

Here are some suggestions for getting the most out of this study guide:

1. Examine the Learning Objectives, Chapter Outline, and People You Should Know prior to reading each chapter of your text. This will give you a basic overview of the information contained in the chapter and will also sensitize you to the most important points that you will encounter during your reading. You may also wish to make a list of the names to remember.

2. After reading the chapter, you should skim through the Learning Objectives and Chapter Outline once again.

3. Try to complete the Matching words and phrases. These will all be key worlds and phrases taken from the chapter. As you read the word or phrase try to formulate a definition prior to looking at the choices. Then, examine the choices to see which, if any, correspond to your definition.

4. Next, try to complete the People: How Much Do You Know? section. Once again, these will be key figures in relation to what you have learned in the chapter. You may wish to re-read the appropriate text material if you have difficulty with this section.

5. Then, complete the Fill-In Questions. Each question is designed to test your knowledge regarding a key point that the author made in the chapter. You may find some of the questions difficult. This is because you will be using the component of memory called "recall" which means that you can remember something without any hints or cues to assist you, as opposed to "recognition" which means that you can recognize the correct answer when you see it (as in multiple-choice questions). If you are able to recall information, you can feel confident that you know the material.

6. The True-False and Multiple-Choice Questions may be used as a final check when preparing to take an exam. After reviewing the material, you might wish to allow yourself a specific time period to answer these questions.

7. Always check you answers carefully against the answers at the end of this study guide. If you find that you have not answered a question correctly, return to your text and re-read at least the entire paragraph containing that information.

8. Finally, you may complete the personal growth exercises. These are optional exercises which have been designed to use the information contained in the text and allow you to apply it to your personal experiences. You may find that some of the exercises do not apply to your present circumstances; however, we feel that many of them will be relevant at some point in your life. As you will discover after reading your text, the more information and understanding you have of yourself and those around you, the more effective you will be in whatever you are attempting to do. Information is the key that unlocks many closed doors.

We hope that the materials contained in this study guide will make a significant contribution to your success in this course, and that this course will make a significant contribution to your success in life.

Sandra L. Dunn
Thomas P. Dunn

CHAPTER 1

Introduction

LEARNING OBJECTIVES

1. Understand the purpose of the textbook and acquire realistic expectations for what reading it can do for you.

2. Identify and define the components of effective behavior.

3. Acquire an appreciation for the scientific approach to the study of behavior.

CHAPTER OUTLINE

I. WELCOME TO PSYCHOLOGY AND EFFECTIVE BEHAVIOR.
   A. Purpose of The Book: to help you learn more about yourself and your world and to use what you learn for more effective behavior.
   B. Unrealistic Expectations: what this book can't do for you:
      1. Make you an expert on human behavior.
      2. Support all of your beliefs.
      3. Solve your problems.
   C. Realistic Expectations: what this book can do for you:
      1. Give you information.
      2. Help you achieve insight (understanding that goes beyond the obvious or simple assumptions or value judgments.
      3. Give you some skills for managing your life more effectively

II. WHAT IS EFFECTIVE BEHAVIOR?
   A. Definition of Effective Behavior: flexible, controlled, and productive behavior that allows you to feel good about yourself and others as you move toward understanding yourself and achieving realistic goals and good relationships.

2   PART 1:

    B. According to the definition, effective behavior incorporates:
       1. Flexible behavior.
       2. Controlled behavior.
       3. Productive behavior.
       4. Self-esteem and self-acceptance.
       5. Self-knowledge.
       6. Realistic personal goals.
       7. Good relationships.
    C. The Psychology of Adjustment.
       1. Constraints put limits on our opportunities and our freedom of action.
       2. Norms (unwritten rules) also place limits on our behavior.
       3. Since constraints and norms provided by ourselves and society serve to regulate our behavior, the subject matter of this course often is called the psychology of adjustment. Common adjustment issues (to which everyone must adjust):
          a. Changing sex role expectations.
          b. Progressive progress.
          c. Advancing medical knowledge.
          d. A more dangerous world.
    D. The Psychology of Effective Behavior.
       1. Finding your own values: values are learned and may be shared with others, but you are free to choose your own.
       2. Choosing a career: you may make an active choice and then feel free to change that choice if it turns out not to suit you.
       3. Choosing a life style: the key is choice and a choice based on your own values allows you to feel in control of your life.
    E. Effective Behavior and a Sense of Control.
       1. Perceived self-efficacy: your belief in your ability to control your own life and cope with your problems.
       2. Learned helplessness: the acquired sense of having little or no control over one's fate.
       3. Belief in your ability to control your own life is a central theme of this book because it is a central aspect of effective behavior.

III. THE SCIENTIFIC STUDY OF HUMAN BEHAVIOR
    A. The science of psychology provides the foundation for this text book.
    B. The Scientific Method: a cyclical process of investigation that is guided by defined rules and logic and is characterized by commonly understood terminology and methods. The sequence of the scientific process is as follows:
       1. Formulate a question.
       2. Make relevant observations.
       3. Draw a conclusion (or inference).
       4. Verify the results.
       5. Replicate the study and make necessary alterations in the inference.

INTRODUCTION 3

    C. The Characteristics of The Scientific Method:
       1. Precise terminology.
       2. Rules for collecting information.
       3. The use of a system of logic to draw conclusions.
       4. The requirement that conclusions be verified.
    D. A Word About Theories.
       1. Definition of a scientific theory: a unified account of some limited range of phenomena.
       2. A good theory must be open to test (although not all theories can be tested in their entirety and some cannot be tested even in part).
       3. When a theory has been so thoroughly tested for so long that there seems no possibility that it will ever be disproved, we speak of a law, such as the law of gravity.
    E. In Conclusion:
       1. Unless it is stated as such, the material in this textbook is not personal opinion.
       2. The conservatism which characterizes the scientific study of behavior can be frustrating, but it protects you from being influenced by untested personal opinions and ideas.
       3. The scientific body of knowledge which provides the basis for this textbook can be of enormous value to you, but the science of psychology cannot give you a formula for achieving the good life. You must work that out for yourself!

REVIEW QUESTIONS

MATCHING: Match the words and phrases below with the definitions

a. effective behavior   f. scientific method
b. learned helplessness   g. personal control
c. insight   h. scientific observations
d. psychology of adjustment   i. constraints on behavior
e. scientific verification   j. self-efficacy

1. **c** Understanding that goes beyond the obvious or simple assumptions or value judgments.
2. **a** Flexible, controlled, and productive behavior that allows you to feel good about yourself and others.
3. **i** Limits on our opportunities and our freedom of action.
4. **d** The subject matter of this course.
5. **j** Your ability to control your own life and cope with your own problems.
6. **b** An acquired sense of having little or no control over one's fate.
7. **f** A cyclical process of investigation that is guided by defined rules and logic and is characterized by commonly understood terminology and methods.
8. **h** Data collected by rules and expressed in a precise vocabulary.

4 PART 1:

9. _e_ Involves the process of replicating studies.
10. _g_ When you seek out your own information about alternatives and make choices based on your own values.

PEOPLE YOU SHOULD KNOW

Seligman
Freud

FILL-IN QUESTIONS

1. The purpose of your text is to help you learn more about yourself and your world and to use what you learn for more _____ _____.

2. Thinking _____ is crucial to managing our lives effectively and sometimes this means facing unpleasant truths.

3. _____ _____ is flexible, controlled, and productive behavior that allows you to feel good about yourself and others as you move toward understanding yourself and achieving realistic personal goals.

4. Each of us lives with _____ that put limits on our opportunities and our freedom of action.

5. Unwritten rules, called _____ also place limits on our behavior.

6. The subject matter of this course often is called the psychology of _____.

7. The list of possible ways to live is quite long despite constraints that might be imposed by your own abilities and life situation. The key is _____.

8. Psychologists and other mental health professionals increasingly are impressed with the role that a sense of _____ plays in physical and mental health and general satisfaction with life.

9. The _____ _____ is a cyclical process of investigation that is guided by defined rules and logic and is characterized by commonly understood terminology and methods.

10. The scientific method uses a system of _____ to draw conclusions.

11. Many research questions come, not from individual curiosity or the research of others, but from _____.

12. The _____ that characterizes the scientific study of behavior can be very frustrating when you want an answer to a question about your life.

13. Science, in particular the science of _____, remains the foundation of this text.

TRUE-FALSE QUESTIONS

T F 1. In order to change someone's behavior, you must change an underlying attitude.

T F 2. Problems can be avoided or solved by thinking positively.

T F 3. Having facts about disturbing problems gives you a perspective that makes them less frightening.

T F 4. Insight is understanding that goes beyond the obvious or simple assumptions or value judgments.

T F 5. The more you understand about yourself and about human behavior the more frustrating life tends to be.

T F 6. Each of us lives with constraints that put limits on our opportunities and our freedom of action.

T F 7. While each of us has a unique personal situation to which to adjust, we also face certain common adjustment issues.

T F 8. Effective behavior is an active concept and there are many aspects of your life in which you can take the initiative and exert this active control.

T F 9. Psychologists use the term perceived self-efficacy to refer to your ability to control your own life.

T F 10. Seligman introduced the term trained incapacity to refer to the acquired sense of having little or no control over one's life.

T F 11. Belief in your ability to control your own life is a central theme of your text because it is a central aspect of effective behavior.

T F 12. To the scientist, nothing is ever proven.

T F 13. Most theories can be tested in their entirety and all theories can be tested in part.

T F 14. Unlike non-scientists, psychologists can give you a formula for achieving the good life.

T F 15. Science, in particular the science of psychology, is the foundation for your text.

PART 1:

MULTIPLE CHOICE QUESTIONS

1. The purpose of your text is to:
   a. show you how positive thinking can help you overcome problems
   b. solve your problems
   c. provide you with a formula for achieving the "good life"
   d. help you learn more about yourself and use what you learn for more effective behavior

2. Which of the following is NOT a characteristic of effective behavior?
   a. other-directedness
   b. flexibility
   c. realism
   d. productivity

3. Which of the following is NOT a common adjustment issue?
   a. changing sex role expectations
   b. progressive progress
   c. a more dangerous world
   d. all of the above are common adjustment issues

4. The scientific method is a cyclical process which begins with a(n)
   a. hypothesis
   b. question
   c. observation
   d. inference

5. Which of the following is NOT a characteristic of the scientific method?
   a. precise terminology
   b. verification of conclusions
   c. absolute, unalterable proof
   d. a system of logic to make inferences

6. A unified account of some limited range of phenomena is known as a(n)
   a. theory
   b. hypothsis
   c. fact
   d. inference

7. Science can best be described as:
   a. liberal
   b. conservative
   c. emotional
   d. absolute

8. The acquired sense of having little or no control over your fate?
   a. ineffective behavior
   b. negative behavior
   c. trained incapacity
   d. learned helplessness

9. Psychologists call your belief in your ability to control your own life and cope with your own problems:
   a. positive thinking
   b. effective behavior
   c. perceived self-efficacy
   d. instrumental behavior

10. When scientists are convinced that their observations are not caused by some chance combination of factors they would say that their observations are:
    a. significant
    b. proven
    c. logical
    d. empirical

11. What kind of behavior are you said to be engaging in when you have your own plans and goals and your own accustomed patterns of behavior but you are not rigid about them and recognize the necessity of being able to adapt to changing conditions?
    a. productive
    b. realistic
    c. flexible
    d. changeable

12. What kind of behavior are you said to be engaging in when you may act impulsively from time to time, but you have confidence in your ability to control your own behavior?
    a. productive
    b. controlled
    c. uncontrolled
    d. unproductive

13. What kind of behavior are you said to be engaging in when you have enthusiasm and energy for life and channel it into activities such as education, work, relationships, and hobbies. You don't have to drive yourself to meet the ordinary demands of daily life?
    a. productive
    b. controlled
    c. realistic
    d. flexible

14. When the wishes of others prevent us from doing something we would like to do, we are giving in to:
    a. norms
    b. laws
    c. expectations
    d. constraints

15. The unwritten rules which place limits on our behavior are known as:
    a. norms

8   PART 1:

    b. laws
    c. expectations
    d. constraints

PEOPLE: HOW MUCH DO YOU KNOW?

Write what you can about the people listed below (as it relates to what you learned in this chapter).

<u>Seligman</u>:

<u>Freud</u>:

PERSONAL GROWTH EXERCISE - WHO ARE YOU?

PURPOSE To help you to understand that the person that you are or that you aspire to be is dependent on the interaction of many variables.

What are your values?

Which of these values are/were also held by your parents?

Which of these values are/were not held by your parents?

What influenced you to hold values not held by your parents?

What sort of life-style do you want for yourself?

Is this the same life-style as that of your parents?

Why, or why not?

What constraints place limits on the way in which you live your life?

What norms place limits on the way in which you live your life?

What expectations do you have for yourself?

PART 1:

What expectations do other people have of you?

Who are those people?

What kinds of conflicts do you encounter due to the expectations of other people?

Would you say that, on the whole, you give in to other people's demands, ignore other people's demands, or that your life consists of a mixture of give-and-take?

(Choosing your own life-style, values and expectations are an important part of the maturation process, but at the same time we must all learn to live within the restrictions placed upon us by society, our own limitations, and the best interest of other people who are important in our life. Learning to balance all of these variables so that you can "be all that you can be" is one of the major goals of this book)

PERSONAL GROWTH EXERCISE - THE SCIENTIFIC METHOD

PURPOSE To acquire an appreciation for the scientific method as a source of valuable information that you can use to develop more effective behavior in your everyday life.

Step One Carefully read the following scenario:

   You have just been arrested and charged with murder. Although there is some circumstantial evidence that makes you a likely suspect, the fact is that you did not kill anyone. You are innocent! At your trial the judge decides to let the jury use whatever method they want in deciding your guilt or innocence. Your lawyer immediately rises to his feet and shouts, "Objection! We demand that the jury use the scientific method in deciding this case."

Step Two Answer each of the following questions in the space provided:

1. What is the scientific method?

2. Do you agree with your lawyer that having the jury use the scientific method is in your best interest? Why or why not? Be sure to consider each of the following in formulating your answer:

   a. The <u>purpose</u> of the scientific method.

   b. The use of <u>precise</u> terminology.

   c. The <u>rules</u> for collecting information.

   d. The use of <u>logic</u> to draw conclusions.

   e. The requirement that conclusions be <u>verified</u>.

   f. The requirement that theories be <u>tested</u>.

   g. The <u>conservative</u> nature of science.

Step Three Think about your responses to the questions above. Would you agree that the scientific method is probably the most reliable means for obtaining <u>facts</u> about social behavior? Why or why not?

CHAPTER 2

You and Your Environment: The Foundations of Behavior

LEARNING OBJECTIVES

1. Acquire a thorough understanding of the nature-nurture controversy.
2. Analyze the complex interrelationship between personal and environmental factors in determining human behavior.

CHAPTER OUTLINE

I. THE NATURE-NURTURE CONTROVERSY
   A. Definition of Psychology: The Study of Human Behavior
      1. Psychology has a long standing tradition of emphasizing the role that individual personal characteristics, especially inherited ones, play in determining behavior
      2. Some psychologists have reconsidered this position and have come to believe that experience with the environment after birth must override inherited characteristics
      3. This debate has come to be known as the nature-nurture controversy
   B. Nature and Nurture Controversy
      1. A debate among scientists and others as to whether heredity or environment plays the greater role in development
      2. Most scientists now agree that both influence behavior
      3. A basic theme of this book is that all behavior is understood only in terms of both personal factors and environmental factors

II. PERSONAL FACTORS AND BEHAVIOR
    A. The mix of genetic and acquired personal characteristics makes up the personal factors that affect behavior
       1. It is not possible to select one set of factors as the most important influence

B. Example: Age and Behavior
   1. Direct effects of age on behavior
      a. Maturation
      b. Puberty
      c. Mental ability
      d. Behavior
   2. Indirect effects of age on behavior
      a. Appearance
      b. Youth culture

III. THE ENVIRONMENT AND BEHAVIOR
  A. The Physical Environment and Behavior
    1. Inherited/biological characteristics form the foundation, but our physical environment (aspects of your surroundings that you can see, smell, feel, and hear) and social environments play a significant role in what kind of people we become and how we behave on a day-to-day basis.
    2. Example: Physical space and behavior
      a. Personal space is an area surrounding the body that we feel belongs to us.
      b. Hall identified four different categories of personal space in American society:
        i. Intimate distance (0-1½ ft.)
        ii. Personal distance (1½-4 ft.)
        iii. Social distance (4-12 ft.)
        iv. Public distance (over 12 ft.)
      c. Density refers to the number of units in a given space.
      d. When there are too many units in a given space we may feel crowded.
  B. **The Social Environment and Behavior**
    1. The social environment consists of other people, our relationships with them, and the laws, rules, and norms that regulate our interactions with them.
    2. Your social environments affect what you can do, what you are expected to do, and what you want to do.
    3. The presence of others and behavior.
      a. The social facilitation effect: the ability of others to bring out the best in our behavior.
      b. The social inhibition effect: occurs when the presence of others interferes with what we are trying to do.
    4. Norms and behavior
      a. Norms are unwritten rules for behavior that grow out of social interaction.
      b. The penalties for violating norms are almost all social
    5. Expectations and behavior
      a. Expectations are beliefs about how another person will, or should, behave.
      b. A self-fulfilling prophecy is the achievement of a particular outcome because one expects it to occur and so behaves in ways that make it "come true"
      c. Your own expectations for yourself also have a signi-

YOU AND YOUR ENVIRONMENT: THE FOUNDATIONS OF BEHAVIOR 15

ficant effect on your behavior
6. The social environment in action: an example
   a. Zimbardo's study of anonymity (the condition of being unknown to those around you)
   b. Social indifference refers to a general lack of interest in, and concern for others in a social environment
   c. The bystander effect refers to an inverse relationship between the number of people who are around when someone is in trouble and the likelihood that this person will help
   d. Example of social indifference and the bystander effect: the Kitty Genovese murder

REVIEW QUESTIONS

MATCHING: Match the words and phrases below with the definitions

a. norms
b. nature-nurture controversy
c. personal space
d. expectations for behavior
e. pygmalion
f. self-fulfilling prophesy
g. social environment
h. social facilitation effect
i. social inhibition effect
j. bystander effect

1. _b_ A debate among scientists and others as to whether heredity or environment plays the greater role in human development and behavior.

2. _c_ An area surrounding the body which we feel belongs to us.

3. _g_ Other people, our relationships with them, and the laws rules, and norms that regulate our interactions with them.

4. _h_ The ability of others to bring out the best in our behavior.

5. _i_ When the presence of others interferes with what we want to do.

6. _a_ Unwritten rules for behavior that grow out of social interaction.

7. _d_ Beliefs about how another person will, or should behave.

8. _f_ The achievement of a particular outcome because one expects it to occur and so behaves in ways that make it "come true."

9. _e_ Synonymous with bringing about change in someone through the way they are treated.

10. _j_ An inverse relationship between the number of people who are around when someone is in trouble and the likelihood that this person will get help.

16 PART 1:

PEOPLE YOU SHOULD KNOW

Huberty	Rosenthal	Latane and Darley
Hall	Zimbardo	
Pessin	Genovese	

FILL-IN QUESTIONS

1. _____ is the study of human behavior.

2. A basic theme of this book is that all behavior is understood only in terms of both _____ factors (which include, but are not limited to, biological factors) and _____ factors.

3. The purpose of this chapter is to help you learn to think of "the cause" of any particular behavior as being made up of a complex _____ of factors.

4. The idea that age is a matter of _____ is not completely true by any means.

5. Spending a great deal of money and time in an effort to look younger is one of the most common _____ effects of age on behavior.

6. Unless conditions are extreme, most of us seldom give much thought to the ways that our _____ environments affect our behavior.

7. _____ refers to the number of units in a given space. When there are too many of these units, be they people or other objects, we may feel _____.

8. To a considerable degree, each of us creates our own _____ environments through our choices of where we live, what people we associate with, and how we spend our time.

9. _____ are unwritten rules for behavior that grow out of social interaction.

10. The penalties for violating norms are almost all _____.

11. _____ are beliefs about how another person will, or should, behave.

12. Research into this theory of work motivation confirms a connection between performance and _____ about performance.

13. _____ definitely appears to be a contributing factor to antisocial behavior, such as vandalizing an automobile.

14. Social _____ refers to a general lack of interest in, and concern for, others in a social environment.

YOU AND YOUR ENVIRONMENT: THE FOUNDATIONS OF BEHAVIOR

TRUE-FALSE QUESTIONS

T F 1. Psychology has a long standing tradition of emphasizing the role that individual personal characteristics, especially inherited ones play in determining behavior.

T F 2. The nature-nurture controversy is a debate among scientists and others as to whether heredity or environment plays the greater role in human development and behavior.

T F 3. Most scientists now agree that the nurture argument is superior to the nature argument in explaining human behavior.

T F 4. Most of the research to date suggests only that certain patterns of individual biological makeup can create a predisposition toward certain behavior patterns.

T F 5. According to your text, human behavior is complex and its causes are multiple and interrelated.

T F 6. Personal factors, both inherited and acquired, influence your behavior at every stage of your life.

T F 7. Although they occur throughout life, the effects of physical and biological age-related changes on behavior are most obvious in people between the ages of 20 and 40.

T F 8. All researchers who have studied differences between older and younger workers have found that the younger ones perform better.

T F 9. For at least a generation, we have lived in a culture that places great value on being young.

T F 10. Most first-time smokers are under the age of 21.

T F 11. Your social environment consists of aspects of your surroundings that you can see, smell, feel, and hear.

T F 12. Personal space is an area surrounding the body that we feel belongs to us.

T F 13. Most people tend to be very aware of their physical environment.

T F 14. The social and physical environments are uncontrollable.

T F 15. Your social environments affect what you can do and what you are expected to do but not what you want to do.

T F 16. The ability of others to bring out the best in our behavior, whether it is work, sports, or just telling a joke, is called

18   PART 1:

the social inhibition effect.

T F 17. Norms are codified (written) rules for behavior that grow out of social interaction.

T F 18. The social facilitation effect is the achievement of a particular outcome because one expects it to occur and so behaves in ways that make it "come true."

T F 19. Your own expectations for yourself have a significant effect on your behavior.

T F 20. Research by Latane and Darley showed that in many situations the more people there are around the less likely it is that a person in need will get help.

MULTIPLE-CHOICE QUESTIONS

1. With respect to the nature-nurture controversy, most psychologists feel that:
   a. nurture is more important than nature
   b. nature is more important than nurture
   c. the nature-nurture debate is meaningless
   d. none of the above

2. The biological change from sexual immaturity to the ability to reproduce is known as:
   a. maturation
   b. puberty
   c. the self-fulfilling prophecy
   d. the pygmalion effect

3. Which of the following effects of aging is more severe in women than in men?
   a. greying hair
   b. redistribution of body fat
   c. thinning hair
   d. developmental bone loss

4. Which of the following is NOT one of Hall's personal distances?
   a. social distance
   b. cultural distance
   c. intimate distance
   d. public distance

5. The number of units in a given space is known as:
   a. density
   b. crowding
   c. social distance
   d. none of the above

YOU AND YOUR ENVIRONMENT: THE FOUNDATIONS OF BEHAVIOR 19

6. The social _____ effect is in evidence when the presence of others interfers with individual performance.
   a. facilitation
   b. psychology
   c. inhibition
   d. bystander

7. Which of the following is NOT one of the important purposes served by norms?
   a. prevent chaos and confusion
   b. help keep groups together
   c. help groups get things done
   d. all of the above

8. Beliefs about how another person will, or should, behave are known as:
   a. norms
   b. expectations
   c. values
   d. attitudes

9. Who, among the following, studied the pygmalion effect in a grade school classroom?
   a. Hall
   b. Zimbardo
   c. Rosenthal
   d. Pessin

10. Who, among the following, introduced the term "bystander effect" to refer to an inverse relationship between the number of people who are around when someone is in trouble and the likelihood that this person will get help?
    a. Latane and Darley
    b. Zimbardo
    c. Rosenthal
    d. Hall

11. What do many researchers consider to be a major factor in producing the bystander effect (as detailed in your text)?
    a. norms
    b. diffusion of responsibility
    c. uncertainty
    d. all of the above

12. On July 18, 1984, an unemployed security guard named James Huberty took a gun into a McDonald's restaurant in Southern California and began shooting. What was the result of this action?
    a. 21 customers were killed and 17 others were injured
    b. Huberty was shot dead by the police
    c. Huberty's widow sued McDonald's
    d. all of the above

20 PART 1:

PEOPLE: HOW MUCH DO YOU KNOW?

Write what you can about the people listed below (as it relates to what you learned in this chapter).

Huberty

Hall

Pessin

Rosenthal

Zimbardo

Genovese

Latane and Darley

YOU AND YOUR ENVIRONMENT: THE FOUNDATIONS OF BEHAVIOR   21

PERSONAL GROWTH EXERCISE - THE YOUTH CULTURE

PURPOSE   To become more aware of how the youth culture in America influences your behavior.

Step One   Briefly describe America's "youth culture" and be sure to note all of the distinctive features.

Step Two   List the products you buy which would identify you with the youth culture.

List 3 things which adolescents do to make them appear older or more mature.

List 3 things which you have done to make yourself appear older.

List 3 things which people do to make them appear younger.

List 3 things which you have done to make yourself appear younger.

PART 1:

Step Three   List 3 things on which you and your parents disagree(d).

Step Four   Are any of the above related to the values and beliefs associated with the youth culture? If so, which ones?

Step Five   Do you think that you will have similar disagreements with your own children (or if you are already a parent, do you already have them)?

Why, or why not?

YOU AND YOUR ENVIRONMENT: THE FOUNDATIONS OF BEHAVIOR

PERSONAL GROWTH EXERCISE - THE POWER OF PERSONAL AND SOCIAL CONSTRAINTS

PURPOSE   To sensitize you to the power of norms and how they influence virtually every aspect of your life.

Step One   Define the following:

1. Norms:

2. Constraints on behavior:

Step Two   Sometime during the next few days make it a point to do at least one, but preferably both, of the following:

1. Make several trips on an elevator while facing the other passengers (the doors should be behind you).

2. The next time a store clerk greets you with the phrase "How are you today?" give them a lengthy and detailed response. Tell them how you are doing physically, socially, and emotionally!

Step Three   Analyze your feelings. How did you feel before, during, and after engaging in the mild forms of deviant behavior?

What were the reactions of the other people in the elevator and/or the store clerk?

It should now be obvious that we live our lives within the confines of enormous social constraints. Who do you believe is more aware of these constraints, people who conform or people who deviate? Justify your answer.

CHAPTER 3

Your Cognitive, Emotional, and Moral Development

LEARNING OBJECTIVES

1. Define cognitive development and acquire a thorough understanding of Piaget's theory of cognitive development.

2. Analyze the process of learning and outline in detail the major aspects of classical conditioning, operant conditioning, and social learning.

3. Define emotion and describe the sequence of events from which emotions are derived.

4. Understand the theories of moral development.

CHAPTER OUTLINE

I. COGNITIVE DEVELOPMENT
   A. Definition of Cognitive Development: the development of your ability to think, learn, solve problems, adapt to your environment, and be creative.
   B. Piaget's Theory of Cognitive Development:
      1. Humans go through a predictable series of cognitive changes as they grow - sensorimotor, preoperational, concrete operations, and formal operations.
      2. Although it has been criticized, Piaget's work remains the standard against which other ideas about early cognitive development are compared.
   C. Learning.
      1. Definition of learning: a relatively permanent change in behavior or behavioral potential that comes about through interaction with the environment.
      2. Classical conditioning: the simplest type of learning

26 YOU: A UNIQUE INDIVIDUAL

         process which comes about through the pairing of a natural
         response with a stimulus that previously had no connection
         with the response.
      3. Operant conditioning: a type of learning which comes about
         through the pairing of some behavior with what happens
         afterwards. It is based on the following consequences:
         a. Punishers: unpleasant consequences of behavior.
         b. Reinforcers: rewarding consequnces of behavior that
            make the same behavior more likely to be repeated in
            the future.
         c. Positive reinforcement: occurs if the reinforcer is of
            a positive nature.
         d. Negative reinforcement: occurs when behavior stops
            something that we find unpleasant, or keeps it from
            happening at all.
         e. Behavior is said to be extinguished when it has left
            your repetoire.
         f. Principles of operant conditioning tell us that you
            will be more effective in erasing the unbecoming be-
            havior of others if you ignore it (neither reinforce
            nor punish).
         g. Thorndike's Law of Effect tells us that learning comes
            about in a systematic way based on experience with the
            environment.
         h. Behaviors that are continuously reinforced are more
            quickly extinguished than those that are intermittently
            reinforced - once the reinforcement is stopped.
      4. Social learning
         a. Definition of social learning: learning from others,
            both from what they say and from what you see them do.
         b. Observational learning is the simplest form of social
            learning and occurs merely by observing what someone
            else (known as a model) does.

II. EMOTIONAL DEVELOPMENT
    A. Emotional Experience: How Do You Know What You Feel?
       1. Emotions are states of feeling characterized by internal
          bodily changes that arise in response to imagined or actual
          events or experiences.
       2. The common sense theory of emotions describes this sequence
          event...emotions...bodily reactions...actions
       3. Most psychologists currently believe that the actual
          sequence is event, bodily reactions, emotion, action.
       4. In this current view, therefore, the emotion does not
          cause the bodily reactions, the reactions cause the emotion
    B. A Theory of Emotional Development.
       1. Greenspan's six-stage theory is the newest model of
          emotional development (see Table 3-5 in your text).
       2. This theory is new and will require more testing before
          firm conclusions can be drawn.
    C. The Concept of Emotional Maturity.

YOUR COGNITIVE, EMOTIONAL, AND MORAL DEVELOPMENT   27

      1. Emotional maturity is a difficult concept to define since it frequently involves value judgments.
      2. Recognizing, owning, accepting and allowing yourself to express your emotions in a nondestructive way are important to your emotional well-being, but there are no objective standards for what you should feel under certain circumstances, or how you should express these feelings.

III. MORAL DEVELOPMENT
    A. Moral Dilemmas
        1. Moral means "of relating to right and wrong"
        2. Moral dilemmas arise when opposing standards for right and wrong are dictating contradictory behaviors.
        3. Frank Herbert believes that most moral dilemmas can be resolved by means of the Golden Rule.
    B. A Theory of Moral Development.
        1. The most well-known theory of moral development was proposed by psychologist Leonard Kohlberg.
        2. Three levels of Kohlberg's theory (see Table 3-7 in text):
           a. Preconventional (birth to 9 years)
           b. Conventional (10 to 15 years)
           c. Postconventional (16 years and older)
        3. Although his theory has been controversial and is not as widely accepted as the theory of Piaget (upon which it is based), Kohlberg's theory is a useful framework for thinking about the complex subject of moral development.
    C. Values.
        1. Definition of values: those aspects of life and living that are important to us personally.
        2. Values have the following uses:
           a. Serve as goals and guidelines for action.
           b. Help you make some tough decisions.
           c. Are part of what defines you as an individual.
        3. Changes in values.
           a. Values are learned and anything that is learned can be changed or modified.
           b. Questioning values, other people's or you own, or even being unsure as to what your own values are, is entirely normal.

REVIEW QUESTIONS

MATCHING: Match the words and phrases below with the definitions

a. classical conditioning
b. cognitive development
c. values
d. emotions
e. extinction of behavior
f. learning
g. moral dilemma
h. operant conditioning
i. negative reinforcement
j. reinforcer

28 YOU: A UNIQUE INDIVIDUAL

1. _b_ Refers to the development of your abilities to think, learn, solve problems, adapt to your environment, and be creative.
2. _f_ A relatively permanent change in behavior or behavior potential that comes about through interaction with the environment.
3. _a_ Comes about through the pairing of a natural response with a stimulus that previously had no connection with the response.
4. _h_ Comes about through the pairing of some behavior with what happens afterwards (the consequences of behavior).
5. _j_ Rewarding consequences of behavior that make it more likely that the same behavior will be repeated in the future.
6. _i_ When behavior stops something that we find unpleasant, or keeps it from happening at all.
7. _e_ When a behavior no longer occurs.
8. _d_ States of feeling characterized by internal bodily changes that arise in response to imagined or actual events or experiences.
9. _g_ When opposing standards for right and wrong are dictating contradictory behaviors.
10. _c_ Those aspects of life and living that are important to us personally.

PEOPLE YOU SHOULD KNOW

Piaget
Pavlov
Thorndike
Bandura

Greenspan and Greenspan
Herbert
Kohlberg

FILL-IN QUESTIONS

1. Psychologists and other scientists who study learning distinguish among several basic types of learning processes. The simplest of these is called _classic_ conditioning.

2. By contrast with punishers, _reinforcers_ are rewarding consequences of behavior that make it more likely that the same behavior will be repeated in the future.

3. When behavior stops something that we find unpleasant, or keeps it from happening at all, we say the behavior has received _negative_ reinforcement.

4. _punishment_ makes it less likely that the behavior will be repeated in the future.

5. The principles of operant conditioning tell us that you will be more effective in erasing this unbecoming behavior by _ignoring_ it.

6. In general, the most stable learning occurs when _continuous_ reinforcement in the early learning stages is gradually reduced to _intermittent_ reinforce-

YOUR COGNITIVE, EMOTIONAL, AND MORAL DEVELOPMENT   29

ment once the behavior is well established.

7. _Moral_ means "of or relating to right and wrong."

8. Frank Herbert, author of the popular Dune series of books, believes that most moral _dilemmas_ can be resolved by means of the Golden Rule: treat other people the way you would want them to treat you.

9. _Values_ are those aspects of life and living that are important to us personally.

10. Right and wrong are concepts that are partially determined by _society_ and partially by _individual_ values.

TRUE-FALSE QUESTIONS

T F 1. Cognitive development refers to the development of your abilities to think, learn, solve problems, adapt to your environment, and be creative.

T **F** 2. Intelligence and cognitive development are the same thing.

T **F** 3. The most famous theory of how cognitive development proceeds in the early years of life was put forth by Frank Herbert.

T F 4. Piaget called the first stage of cognitive development the sensorimotor stage.

T F 5. A child in Piaget's formal operations stage would be capable of hypothetical problem solving.

T F 6. Piaget believed that ALL children go through his stages in the same sequence.

T **F** 7. Learning is a relatively permanent change in behavior or behavior potential that comes about through genetic inheritance.

T **F** 8. The simplest type of learning takes place through social learning.

T **F** 9. Pavlov's study in which he taught a dog to salivate in response to the ringing of a bell is an example of operant conditioning.

T F 10. Operant conditioning comes about through the pairing of some behavior with what happens afterwards.

T F 11. Negative reinforcement is not the same as punishment.

T F 12. Behavior that is a product of continuous reinforcement is more quickly extinguished than that of intermittent reinforcement.

30 YOU: A UNIQUE INDIVIDUAL

T F 13. In the current view of emotions, the emotion does not cause the bodily reactions, the reactions cause the emotions.

TRUE T **F** 14. To say that an adult who throws a temper tantrum is immature is to make a value judgment.

T **F** 15. Most psychologists probably would agree that it is healthy to bottle up feelings or to try to deny that you have them.

T F 16. A moral dilemma arises when opposing standards for right and wrong are dictating contradictory behaviors.

T F 17. The most well-known theory of how we come to develop a sense of right and wrong is that proposed by psychologist Leonard Kohlberg.

T **F** 18. Values make it very difficult to deal with moral dilemmas.

T **F** 19. Once they have been thoroughly established, values cannot be changed.

T F 20. Right and wrong are concepts that are partially determined by society and partially by individual values.

MULTIPLE-CHOICE QUESTIONS

1. Classical conditioning is a learning process associated with the work of:
   a. Piaget
   b. Kohlberg
   c. Pavlov
   d. Greenspan and Greenspan

2. Which of the following is based on the consequences of behavior rather than associations between events?
   a. operant conditioning
   b. classical conditioning
   c. both of the above
   d. none of the above

3. Unpleasant consequences of behavior are called:
   a. positive reinforcement
   b. punishers
   c. negative reinforcement
   d. none of the above

4. The principles of operant conditioning tell us that you will be more effective in erasing unbecoming behavior by _____ it.
   a. reinforcing
   b. punishing
   c. conditioning

    (d.) ignoring

5. Who, among the following, introduced the Law of Effect (the law that tells us that learning comes about in a systematic way based on experience with the environment)?
    a. Kohlberg
    (b.) Thorndike
    c. Piaget
    d. Pavlov

6. Who, among the following, introduced the term "social learning?"
    a. Kohlberg
    b. Piaget
    c. the Greenspans
    (d.) Bandura

7. Which of the following is NOT one of the necessary conditions for social learning to occur?
    a. the learner must be paying attention
    b. the learner must retain what he/she has observed
    (c.) the learner must approve of the behavior
    d. the learner must be motivated to display the behavior

8. States of feelings characterized by internal bodily changes that arise in response to imagined or actual events or experiences are:
    a. reinforcers
    (b.) emotions
    c. values
    d. morals

9. In which of the following situations are values of NO use to you?
    a. setting goals and guidelines for action
    b. making tough decisions
    c. defining yourself as an individual
    (d.) values are of use in all of the above situations

10. Which of the following statements is NOT true?
    a. values are personally important standards
    b. most people have values in common with other people
    c. values may change or shift in priority at any stage of life
    (d.) all of the above statements are true

PEOPLE: HOW MUCH DO YOU KNOW?

Write what you can about the people listed below (as it relates to what you learned in this chapter).

Piaget

32 YOU: A UNIQUE INDIVIDUAL

<u>Pavlov</u>

<u>Thorndike</u>

<u>Bandura</u>

<u>Greenspan and Greenspan</u>

<u>Herbert</u>

<u>Kohlberg</u>

YOUR COGNITIVE, EMOTIONAL, AND MORAL DEVELOPMENT   33

PERSONAL GROWTH EXERCISE - YOUR MORAL DEVELOPMENT

PURPOSE   To gain insight into your present stage of moral development.

Step One   You are a world class athlete who has just been chosen to be a member of the U.S. Olympic team. You have four months left to train. Although your current level of performance is exceptional, your coach feels that unless you improve your performance by taking anabolic steroids you cannot be sure of winning the gold medal. You have been training for many years to achieve this goal, and the enormous financial rewards associated with being an Olympic gold medal winner in this country. Your coach points out that, although they are against the rules of Olympic competition, foreign athletes and even some of your own teammates are using the drugs. He states that the drug, if taken properly for short periods of time, is harmless. However, you have read of some serious side effects. If the steroids are to be effective, you must begin taking them immediately. What will you do?

Step Two   Which of the following statements best sums up the reason for your decision:

1. If I get caught I will be disqualified and lose the medal anyway. I won't take the drugs.

2. I will take the drugs because the rewards of winning are too big not to risk the possible negative consequences.

3. I don't think that it would be wrong to take the drug - it's my body - but it is against the Olympic rules so I will not take the drugs.

4. I am a good person, so I will not take the drugs.

5. The rules are that good athletes don't take drugs, but I have been training for so long and I have spent so much money, and done without so many things, that I deserve that gold medal and all that goes with it. Foreign athletes do it, so I will too. I will take the drugs.

6. So what if everyone else does it. America might hate me for not winning the gold medal when they are expecting me to do so, but I will not take the drugs.

7. Other.

Step Three   Re-read the section in your text which explains Kohlberg's theory of moral development. Which stage does your decision fit into? (see Table 3-7 in the text)

34   YOU: A UNIQUE INDIVIDUAL

PERSONAL GROWTH EXERCISE - LEARNING PROCESSES

PURPOSE   To personalize the learning process.

List 5 attitudes/behaviors/values you have learned via:
a. classical conditioning
   1.
   2.
   3.
   4.
   5.

b. operant conditioning
   1.
   2.
   3.
   4.
   5.

c. social learning
   1.
   2.
   3.
   4.
   5.

Which of these attitudes/behaviors/values play a major part in your life?

Which of these attitudes/behaviors/values play only a minor role in your life?

Can you generalize from your own experiences that one particular method of learning is more effective than the others?

CHAPTER 4

Personality: You as Others See You

LEARNING OBJECTIVES

1. Define personality and describe the subfield of psychology known as personality psychology.
2. Discuss in detail the Trait, Psychodynamic, and Behavioral theories of personality with respect to their major concepts, leading proponents and strengths and weaknesses.

CHAPTER OUTLINE

I. WHAT IS PERSONALITY?
   A. Definition of Personality: the distinctive patterns of behavior (including thoughts and emotions) that characterize each individual's adaptations to the situations of his or her life.
   B. Personality Psychology: an area of study in psychology devoted to describing, measuring, and discovering the sources and meaning of differences in personality.

II. TRAIT THEORIES OF PERSONALITY
   A. Carl Jung believed that introversion and extroversion are fundamental personality traits and that all people are basically either introverts or extroverts.
   B. Gordon Allport believed that your personality is described more accurately in terms of whatever traits are more characteristic of you, not in terms of how much or how little of some predetermined trait you have.
   C. The Meaning of Measurement of Traits
      1. Trait theories begin with the assumption that traits are measurable predispositions to behave in certain ways, with

            each trait constituting a dimension of personality.
         2. Locus of control: a personality trait that many psychologists believe is important in explaining differences in behavior between people.
    D. Traits and Behavior
         1. Personality tests are used for research purposes, for clinical diagnosis, for executive personnel selection, and for vocational guidance.
         2. Research evidence indicates that there is a stable relationship between personality traits and behavior.
    E. Where Do Traits Come From? - most trait theorists believe that traits are developed over time in conjunction with certain basic inherited biological attributes.
    F. Personality Traits and Personality Types
         1. Hippocrates was among the first to believe that personality traits are related to your physical/biological nature.
         2. A personality typology is a system for dividing people into a few categories on the basis of some dominant personality trait.
         3. Jung's introversion-extroversion distinction is one of the first modern personality typologies.

III. PSYCHODYNAMIC THEORIES OF PERSONALITY
    A. Personality According to Freud: Freud viewed personality as being a set of forces made up of the following components:
         1. Id: the core of personality that includes everything of a psychological nature that is present at birth (including the all-important instincts of sex and aggression).
         2. Ego: the part of the personality that responds to the constraints of reality.
         3. Superego: the moral aspect of personality.
         4. Behavior versus personality: a critical and unique feature of Freud's theory is that he believed personality development is complete by age 5 or 6, with subsequent behavior seen as reflecting this earlier development.
    B. Erikson's Psychosocial View of Personality:
         1. Erikson, one of the most influential of Freud's followers, agrees with him that biological development is the fundamental basis for personality development, but disagrees with the premise that sexual urges are all-important.
         2. Erikson places more emphasis on social factors (his theory is often called a psychosocial theory) and posits that people pass through eight definable stages of personality development.
         3. Unlike Freud, Erikson argues that personality continues to develop throughout the life cycle.

IV. BEHAVIOR THEORIES OF PERSONALITY
    A. Focus of Behavior Theories: behavior theories focus on what

PERSONALITY: YOU AS OTHERS SEE YOU   37

   you do; your personality is your behavior.
B. The A-B-C Paradigm:
   1. Antecedents: conditions that prevail prior to the behavior
   2. Behavior: takes place with respect to the antecedents (the sum total of the situation, or context, in which the behavior takes place)
   3. Consequences: what happens after the behavior occurs:
      a. Positive reinforcement: occurs when a desired state of affairs is brought about as a result of the behavior
      b. Negative reinforcement: occurs when a behavior stops something undesirable or keeps it from beginning
      c. Like positive reinforcement, negative reinforcement makes it more likely that the behavior will occur again
      d. Punishment: consists of negative consequences of behaviors which make it less likely that the behavior will be repeated
C. Reinforcers and Punishers:
   1. Learned and unlearned reinforcers:
      a. Learned reinforcers: outcomes of behavior that people have learned to find personally rewarding
      b. Unlearned reinforcers: satisfy some biological need without the necessity for learning
      c. Punishment: unpleasant outcomes of behavior that operate simultaneously with rewards to develop your behavior

V. PUTTING IT ALL TOGETHER
   A. Three very different approaches (Trait, Psychodynamic, and Behavior) to the meaning and development of personality have been reviewed in this chapter.
   B. All three approaches have something to offer you in the matter of trying to understand personality better, both your own and that of others.

REVIEW QUESTIONS

MATCHING: Match the words and phrases below with the definitions

a. cardinal traits
b. secondary traits
c. displacement
d. ego
e. externalizer

f. pleasure principle
g. Freudian slip
h. adolescence
i. A-B-C paradigm
j. antisocial behavior

1. _a_ So general that almost every act of an individual seems to stem from them.
2. _b_ Predispose you to behave in very particular ways in very particular situations that may arise very infrequently.

38 YOU: A UNIQUE INDIVIDUAL

3. _e_ Would prefer to study in locations full of people and noise.
4. _d_ Operates on the reality principle.
5. _f_ The id.
6. _c_ Reduction of tension through a means other than the original choice.
7. _g_ Giving clues to your personality or wishes through certain kinds of behavior mistakes.
8. _h_ Role identity versus role confusion.
9. _i_ A behavioral view of personality examined in terms of what you do, the conditions prevailing when you do it, and what happens as a result.
10. _j_ Behavior that works against the good of society as a whole.

PEOPLE YOU SHOULD KNOW

Monte
Allport
Hippocrates
Jung

Freud
Erikson
Skinner
Mednick

FILL-IN QUESTIONS

1. _personality_ refers to the distinctive patterns of behaviors (including thoughts and emotions) that characterize each individual's adaptations to the situations of his or her life.

2. Allport placed great emphasis on the _individuality_ of personality.

3. _Locus_ of _Control_ is a term used to describe an individual's basic belief about where control over his or her life is located.

4. Is it true that measured personality traits are stable? Reviews of the research evidence tend to _support_ this assumption.

5. Freud viewed personality as being a set of psychological forces that he called the _id_, the _ego_, and the _superego_.

6. _displacement_ refers to the reduction of tension through a means other than the original choice.

7. You give clues to your personality through certain kinds of behavior mistakes, such as the famous Freudian _slip_.

8. _adolescence_ is the time during which a person changes biologically from child to adult.

9. This _identity crisis_, with its uncertainty, confusion, and anxiety, is undoubtedly the most familar of Eriksons concepts.

PERSONALITY: YOU AS OTHERS SEE YOU   39

10. The _antecedents_ of behavior are the conditions that prevail prior to the behavior.

11. Unlearned reinforcers (sometimes called primary reinforcers) satisfy some _biological_ need without the necessity for learning.

12. Like reinforcers, much of what people find punishing is _learned_.

13. Skinner rejects the entire concept of _personality_; he believes that psychology has no need for a separate concept to explain behavior since it can be explained by learning.

14. _Antisocial_ behavior is behavior that works against the good of society as a whole.

15. One thing that all professionals concerned with the problem of antisocial personalities agree on is that it is more effective and more desirable to _prevent_ the development of criminal behavior than it is to try to _change_ it once it has become a way of life.

TRUE-FALSE QUESTIONS

(T) F 1. Personality psychology is an area of study in psychology devoted to describing, measuring, and discovering the sources and meaning of differences in personality.

T (F) 2. Because theories of personality are varied (and frequently in conflict) they are not considered very useful by most of today's psychologists.

(T) F 3. Formal trait theories of personality begin with the assumption that traits are predispositions to behave in certain ways.

(T) F 4. Personality tests are used for research purposes, for clinical diagnoses, for executive personnel selection, and for vocational guidance.

TRUE (F) 5. Your personality, according to trait theorists, developed over time as you interacted with your environment.

T (F) 6. The idea that your personality traits are based partially on your physical/biological nature is relatively new among theories of personality.

T (F) 7. A person with a Type B personality tends to be hurried, compulsive, and less tolerant of the behavior of others than the Type B person.

(T) F 8. Psychodynamic theories focus on postulated internal psychological forces rather than on traits.

40   YOU: A UNIQUE INDIVIDUAL

T (F) 9. According to Freud, the id operates on the pleasure principle while the ego works on the perfection principle.

(T) F 10. A critical and unique feature of the psychodynamic personality theory of Freud is that he believed personality development is complete by age 5 or 6.

(T) F 11. Erik Erikson agrees with Freud that biological development is the fundamental basis for personality development.

(T) F 12. Behavior theories of personality focus on what you do; your personality is your behavior.

(T) F 13. Learned reinforcers are outcomes of behavior that people have learned to find personally rewarding.

TRUE T (F) 14. In general, the effects of punishment on your behavior are more subtle than those of reinforcement.

T (F) 15. Most of those who take a behavioral view of personality development probably would agree that punishers generally have a greater influence on the development of personality than do rewards.

MULTIPLE-CHOICE QUESTIONS

1. Who, among the following, believed that introversion and extroversion are fundamental personality traits and that all people are basically either introverts or extroverts?
    a. Allport
    b. Skinner
    c. Freud
    (d.) Jung

2. Which of the following is a 550 item, true-false, paper and pencil test measuring ten factors among which are paranoia and depression?
    a. California Psychological Inventory
    b. Myers-Briggs Type Indictor
    (c.) Minnesota Multiphasic Personality Inventory
    d. Edwards Personal Preference Schedule

3. Who, among the following, was among the earliest scholars to believe that personality traits are based on a person's physical/biological nature?
    (a.) Hippocrates
    b. Jung
    c. Allport
    d. none of the above

4. A system for dividing people into a few categories on the basis of some dominant personality trait is known as a:
   a. personality theory
   b. personality typology
   c. personality type
   d. trait theory

5. Psychodynamic theories of personality, the first and most famous of which was proposed by _____, focus on postulated internal psychological forces rather than traits.
   a. Gordon Allport
   b. Carl Jung
   c. Sigmund Freud
   d. none of the above

6. Which of the following did Freud believe was the core of personality and includes everything of a psychological nature that is present at birth?
   a. id
   b. ego
   c. superego
   d. displacement

7. According to Freud, which of the following components of personality operated on the principle of perfection?
   a. id
   b. ego
   c. superego
   d. none of the above

8. Who, among the following, proposed a psychosocial theory of personality that suggests that people pass through eight stages of personality development?
   a. Erikson
   b. Jung
   c. Allport
   d. Chance

9. Who, among the following, would most likely utilize the A-B-C paradigm in analyzing personality?
   a. a psychodynamic theorist
   b. an Eriksonian analyst
   c. a behavioral theorist
   d. a trait theorist

10. Reinforcers and punishers are best described as _____ of behavior.
    a. antecedents
    b. consequences
    c. shadowers
    d. compliments

42 YOU: A UNIQUE INDIVIDUAL

PEOPLE: HOW MUCH DO YOU KNOW?

Write what you can about the people listed below (as it relates to what you learned in this chapter).

Monte

Allport

Hippocrates

Jung

Freud

Erikson

PERSONALITY: YOU AS OTHERS SEE YOU   43

Skinner

Mednick

44   YOU: A UNIQUE INDIVIDUAL

PERSONAL GROWTH EXERCISE - DO YOU SEE YOURSELF AS OTHERS SEE YOU?

PURPOSE   To gain insight into the impression you are making on others.

1. List 10 of your most positive personality traits.

   1.   6.
   2.   7.
   3.   8.
   4.   9.
   5.   10.

2. Ask 3 people who are close to you to make a list of 10 of your positive personality traits.

3. Compare the lists as follows:

   a. Which, if any, traits appeared on all three of your evaluator's lists?

   b. Which, if any, of these traits also appeared on your own self-evaluation?

   c. Did anyone else's list closely approximate your own?

                    yes _____   no _____

   d. If yes, why do you think this happened? (Does that person know a great deal about you or very little?)

   e. If no, why do you think that this occurred?

4. Overall, does it appear that others see you as you see yourself?

                    yes _____   no _____

5. If no, how can you change your behavior so that others will perceive you as you wish to be perceived?

PERSONAL GROWTH EXERCISE - YOUR PERSONALITY

PURPOSE To help you to understand the etiology of some of your own basic behavior traits.

Step One List 5 behavior traits that you posses
1.
2.
3.
4.
5.

Step Two Using the A-B-C paradigm discussed in this chapter, can you think of the antecedents and consequences which led you to acquire and to maintain these behavior traits?

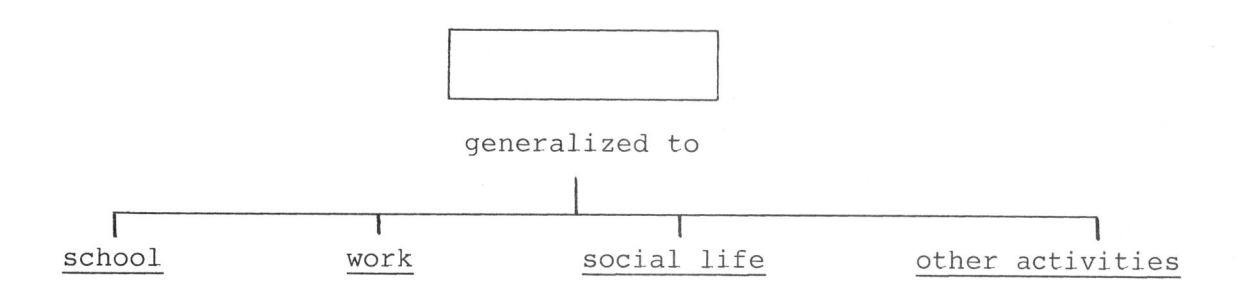

```
        ┌─────────────┐
        │             │
        └─────────────┘
         generalized to
    ┌────────┬────────┬────────┐
  school    work   social life   other activities
```

CHAPTER

5 The Self and Self-Concept: You as You See Yourself

LEARNING OBJECTIVES

1. Define self and discuss its relationship to personality.

2. Present a detailed analysis of the humanistic view of personality as epitomized by the work of Abraham Maslow and Carl Rogers.

3. Define self-concept and describe the process by which it is acquired

4. Differentiate between self-concept, the ideal self, and self-esteem and outline the process by which self-esteem can be changed.

CHAPTER OUTLINE

I. WHAT IS A SELF?
   A. Definition of Self: your consciousness of being a complex entity that is separate from the world around you.
   B. Self and Personality
      1. Social self: the face and behavior you present to others
      2. Personal self: the self seen by you alone
      3. Your self is not the same as your personality, but your personality is an important part of your self

II. THE HUMANISTIC VIEW OF PERSONALITY
   A. Humanistic Personality Theory: a major theoretical approach to the study of personality which argues that the core of personality is an individual's own personal subjective view of being human.
   B. Maslow and Self-Actualization
      1. Maslow believed that people are born with an active

48 YOU: A UNIQUE INDIVIDUAL

          impulse to grow into healthy, happy humans.
       2. Maslow postulated two sets of needs:
          a. Basic needs: physiological needs
          b. Metaneeds: needs for more abstract states
       3. He also believed that the needs have a set order of importance (need hierarchy) as follows: physical, safety, love and belongingness, esteem, self actualization (see Figure 5-1 in the text)
       4. Self actualization is the need to be all that you are personally capable of being as a human being
       5. Most people are not self-actualizers in the pure sense
    C. Rogers' Self Theory of Personality
       1. Carl Rogers, a humanistic psychologist, believed the self, not traits or psychological forces, is the core of personality
       2. Unconditional positive regard means receiving acceptance, love, and esteem from another without having to meet some standards (called conditions of worth) that he or she imposes upon you
       3. The Good Me and Bad Me: the problem with believing in a good me and a bad me is that we begin to distort or deny having feelings or doing things that our parents (and/or parent substitutes) disapprove of (the bad me in action) because we are afraid we will lose their love if they find out
       4. Self-theory and the well-adjusted personality: the fewer the conditions of worth a person has acquired, the more well-adjusted he or she is likely to be
       5. Rogers' beliefs about self-acceptance are at the heart of his well-known humanistic approach to psychotherapy which he called client-centered therapy

III. YOUR SELF CONCEPT
    A. Definition of Self-Concept: your impression of yourself
    B. Development of Your Self-Concept:
       1. Parents and your self-concept: Rogers believed that parents are the most important influences on how self-concept develops
       2. Peers, friends, and your self-concept: the influences of peers and friends are second only to those of parents in the development of the self-concept
       3. When people who are important to us have different ideas about what is desirable and acceptable behavior we can experience what Leon Festinger called cognitive dissonance (which occurs when one fact or belief conflicts with other facts or beliefs
       4. Society and your self-concept: the values of a society lead to the formation of a stereotype (a generalized idea about how people of a given sex, race, or other grouping do or should behave, think, feel, and look) which can have

THE SELF AND SELF-CONCEPT: YOU AS YOU SEE YOURSELF

a strong influence on individual self-concepts as well
5. Physical appearance and self-concept: stereotypes of attractiveness are very poor influences on the self-concept of men and women who do not meet them
6. Sex roles and self-concept:
   a. Definition of sex role: a collection of behaviors considered appropriate for men or women in a particular society or segment of society
   b. The world begins teaching us our sex roles the day we are born
   c. Gender identity: refers to a personal sense of being male or female. It is acquired in large part during the socialization process (the process by which an individual acquires the values and learns the behavior expected in a particular society)
7. Sex role stereotypes: beliefs about basic differences between males and females that do not hold up to scientific investigation. There is no evidence that they are true for men and women in general
8. Gender identity, sex roles, and self-concept: people tend to describe themselves relative to social expectations about their sex. This tendency is greater among those who have a very strong sense of gender identity and accept the traditional sex-role stereotypes

IV. SELF-CONCEPT, THE IDEAL SELF, AND SELF-ESTEEM
   A. The Ideal Self: the picture a person has of the way he/she would like to be. Measures of the discrepancy between self and ideal self are helpful when people are dissatisfied with themselves or their lives
   B. The Self and Self-Esteem
      1. Definition of self-esteem: your evaluation of your self-concept, that is, how highly you regard yourself
      2. People who believe that they are not as good as other people are said to have an inferiority complex
      3. Changing self-esteem: low self esteem begins early, but there is no limit on raising it again
      4. Self-esteem and self-talk:
         a. Unlike other psychologists, Ellis believes that many problems are the result of irrational beliefs about the world (which develop well beyond childhood)
         b. Ellis believes that these irrational beliefs lead us to "talk crazy" to ourselves when interpreting our experiences
         c. To counteract such irrational thinking, Ellis developed what he calls rational emotive therapy, in which the therapist's job is to help people to think more rationally about their experiences

50 YOU: A UNIQUE INDIVIDUAL

REVIEW QUESTIONS

MATCHING: Match the words and phrases below with the definitions

a. androgyny
b. basic needs
c. cognitive dissonance
d. conditions of worth
e. ideal-self
f. incongruence
g. irrational beliefs
h. metaneeds
i. prepotent needs
j. self-concept

1. _b_ Physiological needs (food, shelter), safety needs, belongingness needs, needs for esteem from self and others, and a need to develop fully as a human being.
2. _h_ Needs for more abstract states, such as needs for truth, justice, perfection, and beauty.
3. _i_ Unmet needs lower in the need hierarchy which exert the most influence on behavior until they are satisfied.
4. _d_ Standards imposed upon people before they may receive acceptance and love from certain other people.
5. _f_ Discrepancy between self-image and experience with the world.
6. _j_ Your impression of yourself.
7. _c_ Occurs when one fact or belief conflicts with other facts or beliefs about the same subject.
8. _a_ Displaying both male and female characteristics.
9. _e_ A picture a person has of the way he/she would like to be.
10. _g_ Lead people to set standards for themselves that are so unrealistic they cannot possibly live up to them.

PEOPLE YOU SHOULD KNOW

Maslow
Rogers
Festinger
Cash and Janda

Jourard
Ellis
Sadker and Sadker

FILL-IN QUESTIONS

1. Your _self_ is your consciousness of being a complex entity that is separate from the world around you.

2. To Rogers, a therapist's primary responsibility is to create a climate of warmth and acceptance through _empathy_ with a client's view and experiences.

3. Humanistic personality theorists also differ from the other major approaches in their definite and consistent emphasis on the _positive_ aspects of human nature.

4. If your parents are the most important influence on your self-

THE SELF AND SELF-CONCEPT: YOU AS YOU SEE YOURSELF 51

concept, your _peers_ and _friends_ are not far behind.

5. A _stereotype_ is a generalized idea about how people of a given sex, age, race, or other grouping should or do behave, think, feel, and look.

6. The causes of the more extreme forms of cross gender identity (_transsexualism_) are not well understood.

7. Most adults who are asked to provide self-descriptions will begin by identifying their _sex_ and many other aspects of their descriptions may be related to this one.

8. _Androgyny_, whether physical, psychological, or both, simply means displaying both male and female characteristics.

9. Your self is your _consciousness_ of being a person who is separate from your environment. Your self-concept is your _description_ of this self.

10. Your _self-esteem_ is your evaluation of your self-concept, that is, how highly you regard yourself.

TRUE-FALSE QUESTIONS

T (F) 1. Most people are born with a sense of self.

(T) F 2. Humanistic theorists believe that an individual's own personal subjective view of being human is the most important aspect of personality.

(T) F 3. Abraham Maslow endorsed a humanistic view of personality development.

(T) F 4. Maslow believed that people are born with an active impulse to grow into healthy, happy humans.

T (F) 5. According to Maslow, basic needs include the needs for truth, justice, perfection, and beauty.

(T) F 6. Self actualization is the need to be all that you personally are capable of being as a human being.

(T) F 7. Like other humanistic theorists, psychologist Carl Rogers believed that the self is the core of personality.

T (F) 8. Unconditional positive regard includes the conditions under which another person will care for you.

T (F) 9. According to Rogers, the more conditions of worth a person has acquired, the more well-adjusted he or she is likely to be.

52 YOU: A UNIQUE INDIVIDUAL

(T) F 10. Rogers' humanistic approach to psychotherapy is known as client-centered therapy.

(T) F 11. Rogers believed that parents (and/or parent substitutes) are the most important influences on how self-concept develops.

(T) F 12. Cognitive dissonance occurs when one fact or belief conflicts with other facts or beliefs about that same subject.

(T) F 13. A stereotype is a collection of behaviors considered appropriate for men or women in a particular society or segment of society. *False*

(T) F 14. Socialization is the process by which an individual acquires the values and learns the behaviors expected in a particular society or subgroup of society.

(T) F 15. Gender identity refers to a personal sense of being male or female.

(T) F 16. Research by developmental psychologists find that most children have acquired some sense of gender identity by the age of three.

T (F) 17. Beliefs about basic differences between males and females that have been verified by empirical research are known as sex-role stereotypes.

(T) F 18. One of the most dramatic differences Sadker and Sadker found when they studied teacher behavior was the different way teachers responded to children in classroom discussion.

T (F) 19. Most adults who are asked to provide self descriptions will begin by identifying their occupation.

T (F) 20. The social self is a picture a person has of the way he or she would like to be.

MULTIPLE-CHOICE QUESTIONS

1. A person's earliest conceptions of me/not me are:
    a. psychological
    b. social
    (c.) physical
    d. cultural

2. The humanistic psychologist who identified two sets of needs (basic and metaneeds) was:
    (a.) Maslow
    b. Ellis

c. Rogers
   d. Festinger

3. Which of the following was NOT included in the hierarchy of needs.
   a. safety
   b. esteem
   c. physical
   d. social

4. The phrase "You're a good boy" would be called a(n) _____ by Carl Rogers.
   a. unconditional positive regard
   b. condition of worth
   c. metaneed
   d. ideal self

5. Who, among the following, introduced the concept of cognitive dissonance?
   a. Festinger
   b. Rogers
   c. Jourard
   d. Ellis

6. Who, among the following, is known for doing research which shows that physical characteristics can influence such things as grades in school and selection for jobs?
   a. Jourard
   b. Cash and Janda
   c. Sadker and Sadker
   d. none of the above

7. The personal sense of being male or female is known as:
   a. gender
   b. gender identity
   c. a sex role
   d. cognitive dissonance

8. Which of the following statements is False?
   a. Most antisocial personalities are men
   b. More women attempt suicide, but more men succeed in taking their own lives
   c. Women are more conservative when it comes to sexual attitudes than men
   d. All of the above are true

9. A person who displays both male and femal characteristics would best be termed:
   a. transsexual
   b. incongruent
   c. androgynous
   d. empathetic

54 YOU: A UNIQUE INDIVIDUAL

10. Who, among the following, is known for developing "rational emotive therapy?"
    a. Rogers
    b. Maslow
    c. Jourard
    d. none of the above

PEOPLE: HOW MUCH DO YOU KNOW?

Write what you can about the people listed below (as it relates to what you learned in this chapter).

Maslow

Rogers

Festinger

Cash and Janda

Sadker and Sadker

Jourard

Ellis

56   YOU: A UNIQUE INDIVIDUAL

PERSONAL GROWTH EXERCISE - YOUR OWN NEEDS HIERARCHY

PURPOSE   To help you to determine how you allocate your time to meeting various types of needs.

Step One   Keep a detailed diary of your behavior during a typical weekday. Make an entry every hour, and try to record everything you did during that hour.

Step Two   List below, in order, the needs contained in Maslow's hierarchy of needs.

1. _____:

2. _____:

3. _____:

4. _____:

5. _____:

Step Three   Assign each of the behaviors in your diary to one of the above catagories of need.

Step Four   Carefully analyze the data in step three:
a. Which of the needs appear to occupy most of your time?
b. Does your behavior correspond to Maslow's beliefs about the order in which needs are met?
c. Would your behavior on weekends be substantially different?
d. Do you think that the present pattern of meeting your needs will hold true in the future?
e. Will future changes be positive?
f. Why, or why not?

Step Five   Based on Maslow's idea of a self-actualizing person defined in Exhibit 5-2 of your text, are you a self-actualizing person?

If not, what can you do to become more of a self-actualizer?

THE SELF AND SELF-CONCEPT: YOU AS YOU SEE YOURSELF   57

PERSONAL GROWTH EXERCISE - SELF-CONCEPT

PURPOSE   To increase your awareness of your self-concept and how it was acquired.

Step One   Answer the question "What kind of person are you?" by listing at least 15 characteristics that you feel best describe you.

Step Two   According to your text, our images of ourselves come "from comparing ourselves to others and from the way that we interpret others' expectations and reactions to our behavior." With this in mind, who were the key people whose expectations and reactions most influenced you concerning each of the above characteristics?

Step Three   Analyze your answers to step two:

a. How many of the characteristics were influenced by your mother? _____
b. How many of the characteristics were influenced by your father? _____
c. How many were influenced by a grandparent? _____
d. How many were influenced by another relative? _____   Who? _____
e. How many were influenced by friends you no longer have? _____
f. How many were influenced by friends you have now? _____
g. How many were influenced by teachers? _____
h. How many were influenced by a religious leader? _____
i. How many were influenced by a politician? _____
j. How many were influenced by your socio-economic group? _____
k. How many were influenced by society? _____   What aspect of society?
_____
l. Other influences _____

(Ideally, there should be several diverse influences in your life)

Step Four   With these thoughts in mind, how actively will you monitor the expectations and reactions that your own children (will) receive?

CHAPTER 6

Your Social World: Attraction and Friendship

LEARNING OBJECTIVES

1. Become aware of and understand the reasons for interpersonal attraction.
2. Define friendship, and recognize what qualities you look for in a friend and what qualities you bring to your friendships.
3. Understand the importance of social relationships and stress.

CHAPTER OUTLINE

I. THE DEVELOPMENT OF YOUR SOCIAL SELF
   A. The Importance of Attachment
      1. Attachment: a term psychologists use to describe the bonds that people form with others
         a. First formed to mother, father and/or other primary care giver
         b. Next, playmates and classmates
         c. Later, personal relationships with members of both sexes
         d. Finally, we may find one special relationship and marry and have children too
      2. Human infants are helpless and need comfort, protection, and the physical necessities to sustain life and grow
      3. Secure relationships provide a secure base for young children from which they may venture out and explore the world
      4. Form and reasons for attachments become more complex as we grow older
      5. Critical period: birth to 3 years
         a. Positive attachment seems to be the basis for later childhood social interaction

            b. Research does not prove that infants not able to form attachments experience more social difficulties as adults
        6. Securely-attached children (those who formed close attachments to adults as infants:
            a. Respond more positively to strangers in the toddler stage
            b. Are less hesitant about exploring their world
            c. Are more likely to be group leaders among peers
        7. Close mother-daughter relationships lead to child's close relationships with other girls
        8. The adult needs of recognition, esteem, understanding, and sex are dependent on other people for fulfillment
        9. Qualities adults want in friends:
            1. Trustworthiness, loyalty, affection/warmth
            2. Supportiveness, frankness, sense of humor
            3. Willing to make time for a friend, independence
            4. Least important (of choices given): similar income and/or occupation
    B. Peers and Peer Groups
        1. Definition of peer: all age mates
        2. Definition of peer groups: subsets of this larger group of age-mates
            a. Basis for kindergarten peer group formation: sitting together in class or on school bus
            b. Early peer groups comprise same-sex members and have a limited role
        3. Peer acceptance:
            a. Having an acknowledged role in the same-age social system
            b. Very important
            c. Provides not only friends but "a place to be" in the overall scheme of things
            d. Becomes more important and more complex as the child grows older
            e. 8-year olds - dress alike and giggle at the same time
            f. 10 year olds - must have similar likes and dislikes, and be willing to go along with group ideas
            g. Teenagers - dress code, norms, sanctions, language
        4. Adolescent peer groups:
            a. Acceptance is critical to mature social relationships
            b. Support and guidance prior to complete independence
        5. Peer group influence:
            a. Negative influences concern parents (drugs, unwise or dangerous activities)
            b. Psychologists believe: real standards that are fair and consistantly applied help counteract negative peer influences
            c. Vulnerability to peer pressure is not peculiar to teenagers
    C. Social Relationships and Stress

YOUR SOCIAL WORLD: ATTRACTION AND FRIENDSHIP 61

       1. Social relationships may serve as a buffer against the negative effects of stress
       2. Stanley Schachter experiment:
          a. Undergraduate women exposed to a high stress situation reported a strong desire for others during a waiting period
          b. More than twice the preference than in a low stress situation
          c. Strongest in older daughters
          d. Not true for men in the same situations
          e. Opened a new approach to the study of stress management
  D. Social Support: a complexity of positive effects that an individual may experience as the result of being part of a network of personal relationships (friends, family, neighbors)
       1. Researchers do not agree on the relationship between stress and social support:
          a. It may reduce the perception of stress
          b. It may help people cope with stress
       2. Kobasa's <u>hardy personality</u>: is a positive and optimistic person who may be more actively involved in seeking and successful in attaining a social support system
       3. Practical assistance from social support:
          a. Tangible support: to <u>do</u> something for you
          b. Information: to solve the problem and/or to show that your situation or your fears are not unique
          c. Emotional support: someone who will listen
  E. Support Groups: formed for the purpose of providing mutual support to people coping with the same problem
       1. Types: loss of a child, spouse, or parent; unemployment; disease; alcoholism; divorce
       2. For information: contact your local mental health agency, family service agency, hospital health education office, college counseling office, or look in your local phone directory
       3. All groups provide emotional support (from others who have experienced the same problem) and information about additional resources

II. INTERPERSONAL ATTRACTION: THE FOUNDATION OF SOCIAL LIFE
  A. Social Interaction: the term used to describe encounters and relationships with others
       1. Provide: stimulation, help in meeting a variety of needs, models to imitate or avoid, buffers against stress
       2. Norms:
          a. Unwritten rules for behavior
          b. Not fixed, but change as society changes
          c. Highly sensitive to the social environment
          d. "Encounters" - norms dictate how you behave during brief social meetings

- B. Interpersonal Attraction: you select your partners for special relationships on the basis of your attraction to them
- C. Attraction: a feeling of being drawn to another person:
    1. Attractive or not
    2. Same or opposite sex
    3. Young or old
- D. Factors that Influence Attraction:
    1. Proximity: all other things being equal, the most important factor influencing your choice of partners for social relationships is geographical proximity (nearness)
    2. Functional distance: practical distance (how easy is it to interact with people face-to-face - the closer the better for social relationships to develop
        a. Familiarity does not breed contempt unless your initial reactions to someone are quite negative
    3. Similarity: of backgrounds, interests, and attitudes increase the strength of interpersonal attraction:
        a. Attitude similarity: consistently shown to increase attraction
        b. Complementary hypothesis: opposites attract, but only when dealing with personality characteristics (as opposed to attitudes)
        c. Physical attractiveness: evidence shows that relationships between people of about the same level of physical attractiveness seem to fare best
    4. Reciprocity: persons with a tendency to express feelings of interest or liking, or to return compliments, will be more likely to be seen as attractive (unless false or overdone)
- E. What Makes People Attractive?
    1. A positive first impression
    2. Good-looking people are seen by others to be more intelligent, interesting, competent, sensitive, modest, kind, poised, and sociable than physically unattractive people
        a. Except for intelligence this may be true because attractive people receive more positive reinforcement and this brings out the best in people
    3. "Born beautiful" - bone structure, coloring, body build, regular features etc. (most people try to improve on this)
    4. Psychologists have found that other factors influence the way people judge appearance:
        a. Happy expression
        b. The company you keep (ordinary looking women were judged more attractive when in the company of very attractive women than when seen with unattractive women)
        c. The expected relationship: if purely sexual, then physical features will be important, but if interested in a long-term relationship an attractive personality character, and behavior are more important
        d. Other people's evaluations are important in your per-

YOUR SOCIAL WORLD: ATTRACTION AND FRIENDSHIP   63

            ception of attractiveness
        e. Maybe first impressions should not be so important after all
    F. The Development of a Relationship
        1. According to Levinger, relationships move through a series of predictable stages:
            a. Stage 1: Zero Contact - the parties are unaware of one another's existence
            b. Stage 2: Awareness - both people have seen each other but no contact has been made
            c. Stage 3: Surface Contact - "encounters"
                i. "small talk"
                ii. exploration of similarity and reciprocity
                iii. self disclosure - if interpersonal attraction increases you go on to:
            d. Stage 4: Mutuality - "we-ness" develops either as just a close friendship or more
        2. Self-disclosure and a developing relationship:
            a. Self-disclosure: the sharing of personal information
            b. Women are usually more self-disclosing than men, and women also tend to form closer same-sex relationships than men
            c. Early disclosers: those who tell too much too soon are seen as less secure, less sincere, less mature, and more self-absorbed than late disclosers, and this tends to turn people off (especially men)
            d. Standards for self-disclosure:
                i. facts and preferences
                ii. strong opinions
                iii. emotional or negative personal information
                iv. secrets

III. THE NEED FOR INTIMACY
    A. Definition of Intimacy: a need for very close personal, and meaningful interaction with another person on a physical, emotional, and/or intellectual level
    B. Friendship/Friends:
        1. Among our most valuable assets
        2. Provide companionship, support and a "sounding board"
        3. Cheer us up and comfort us
        4. Provide practical help in various circumstances
    C. What Do You Look For In a Friend?
        1. Certain qualities are valued by many people - trustworthyness, loyalty, affection
        2. Frankness increases trust
        3. Supportiveness reduces competition
        4. Independence reduces one-sided domination
        5. A sense of humor helps during rough times
        6. Being a friend is an important part of having a friend
    D. Being a Friend:

64 YOUR WORLDS

1. Be appreciative and thoughtful
2. Keep in touch
3. Be alert for signals
4. Do it, don't just offer!
5. Don't pretend or lie
6. Don't be a user

REVIEW QUESTIONS

MATCHING: Match the words and phrases below with the definitions

a. attachment
b. early disclosers
c. encounter
d. self-disclosure
e. proximity and attraction
f. reciprocity and attraction
g. similarity and attraction
h. social support
i. support group
j. social interaction

1. _a_ The bonds that people form with others.
2. _h_ A complexity of positive effects that an individual may experience as the result of being part of a network of personal relationships.
3. _i_ Formed for the purpose of providing mutual help to people coping with the same problem.
4. _j_ The term used to describe your encounters and relationships with others.
5. _e_ The most important factor influencing your choice of partners.
6. _g_ When having the same background, interests, values, and attitudes affect the way you feel about someone.
7. _f_ The tendency to return compliments or express feelings of interest or liking.
8. _c_ When "small talk" is most likely to occur.
9. _d_ The sharing of personal information with another person.
10. _b_ Seen as less secure, sincere, mature; and more self-absorbed.

PEOPLE YOU SHOULD KNOW

Kobasa
Levinger
Schachter

FILL-IN QUESTIONS

1. _attachment_ is the term psychologists use to describe the bonds that people form with others.

2. Many psychologists believe that the time between birth and three years of age is a _critical period_ for human social development.

YOUR SOCIAL WORLD: ATTRACTION AND FRIENDSHIP 65

3. In a social development sense, _peers_ are age-mates, and _peer groups_ are subsets of this larger group.

4. _Adolescence_ can be a trying time, you are simultaneously too old and too young.

5. One theory is that social support acts as a _buffer_ against stressful circumstances and events.

6. _Support groups_ are formed for the purpose of providing mutual help to people coping with the same problem.

7. Between __15__ and __35__ percent of the population in this country is in need of mental health services at any given time.

8. _Involuntary attachments_ include volunteer work, foster care, joining clubs, taking lessons, and getting a pet.

9. _Social interaction_ is the term used to describe your encounters and relationships with others.

10. Three factors found to be important in attraction are _proximity_, _similarity_, and _reciprocity_.

11. Often people, especially males, have less interest in pursuing a relationship with a(n) _early_ discloser.

TRUE-FALSE QUESTIONS

T (F) 1. According to a 1979 <u>Psychology Today</u> survey, respondants felt that two of the most important qualities of friendship were similar income and similar occupation.

(T) F 2. Attachment is a term psychologists use to describe the bonds that people form with others.

(T) F 3. Children who formed close attachments to adults as infants have been found to respond more positively to strangers when they are toddlers.

T (F) 4. Young peer groups are usually mixed-sex groups, but this changes when the children reach 7 or 8 years of age.

T (F) 5. Adolescent peer groups are the most important influence for teens and this influence cannot be counteracted by parents or teachers.

(T) F 6. The term social support refers to a complexity of positive effects that an individual may experience as the result of being part of a network of personal relationships.

66   YOUR WORLDS

T (F) 7. Support groups are formed for the purpose of providing ~~help~~ to people coping with the same problem.   *mutual support*

(T) F 8. The need for peer acceptance usually peaks during the teenage years.

(T) F 9. Norms are unwritten rules for behavior that grow out of social interaction, and change as society changes.

↑ T (F) 10. Other things being equal, the most important factor influencing your choice of partners for social relationships is geographical proximity.

T (F) 11. Functional distance and geographical distance are the same.

T (F) 12. The complimentary hypothesis of interpersonal attraction is based on the idea that attitude similarity increases attraction.

(T) F 13. Many studies have shown that good-looking people are perceived by others to be more interesting, competent, sensitive, modest, kind, poised and sociable than physically unattractive people, and they may <u>in fact</u> be more likely to posses these qualities.

(T) F 14. According to Levinger, if a person finds another person's "small talk" interesting and attractive, they will gradually move on to disclose secrets about themselves.

T (F) 15. A need for intimacy refers to a person's sexual needs.

F T (F) 16. There is a great deal of evidence to suggest that children who are not able to form secure attachments during the critical period from birth to age three years have problems with relationships later in life.

(T) F 17. In a high school graduating class, your peers are a larger group than your peer group.

MULTIPLE-CHOICE QUESTIONS

1. Infants form their first strong attachment to their primary caregiver because they are:
   a. human
   (b.) helpless
   c. lovable
   d. happy

2. Which of the following qualities was NOT regarded as the <u>most</u> valued in a friend, in a survey conducted by <u>Psychology Today</u>?
   a. trustworthiness
   b. loyalty

c. affection
   d. *sense of humor*

3. The critical period for human social development is felt to last from:
   a. *birth to age 3*
   b. birth to age 5
   c. birth to age 8
   d. age 3 to age 7

4. Having an acknowledged role in the same-age social system is known as:
   a. peer group formation
   b. peer group role
   c. *peer acceptance*
   d. age-mate role

5. At what age does the expression of similar likes and dislikes and being willing to go along with group ideas about what to do with time become an important part of the price of acceptance in peer groups?
   a. *10*
   b. 12
   c. 14
   d. 15

6. Many psychologists believe that parents and teachers are able to counter the more negative effects of peer group influence in the long run. How?
   a. *with real standards that are fair and consistently enforced*
   b. with strict discipline
   c. by monitoring peer group relationships
   d. with long, regular heart-to-heart talks with the child

7. According to Schachter, _____ appears to help many people feel less overwhelmed by certain kinds of stressful pressures, frustrations, and problems.
   a. self-disclosure
   b. *social support*
   c. alcohol
   d. counseling

8. _____ may be more active in seeking social support and may be more successful in attaining social support.
   a. a good-looking person
   b. a person with a serious problem
   c. securely-attached people
   d. *the hardy personality*

9. Members of a social support network can provide information when you have a problem which will show you that your situation or your

fears are:
a. your own fault
b. someone else's fault
c. not unique ✓
d. the fault of society

10. _____ groups are formed for the purpose of providing mutual aid to people coping with the same problem.
a. therapy
b. D.A.S.
c. peer
d. support ✓

11. The foundation of social life is:
a. the family
b. interpersonal attraction ✓
c. the mutuality stage of relationship development
d. functional acceptance

12. If everyone trained at the doctoral and the master's degree level in the field of mental health services devoted <u>all</u> of their professional time to working with those who need mental health services (15 -35 percent of the population), how much time would each client receive?
a. six hours a year ✓
b. twelve hours a year
c. twenty-four hours a year
d. twenty-eight hours a year

13. According to your text, _____ has been found to be a source of significant positive support for elderly women.
a. going to church ✓
b. giving cooking lessons to young people
c. mall-walking
d. BACCUS of the U.S.A.

14. Unwritten rules of social behavior that grow out of social interaction are called:
a. attitudes
b. mores
c. norms ✓
d. regulations

15. Which of the following is NOT mentioned in your text as being an important aspect of the attraction one person feels for another?
a. proximity
b. respectability ✓
c. similarity
d. reciprocity

16. <u>When it comes to attitudes</u>, relevant research leaves little doubt:

a. similarity increases attraction
b. opposites attract
c. geographical distance is important
d. reciprocity makes one more attractive

17. The _____ of interpersonal attraction is based on the idea that people tend to seek out in others those traits they find desirable but lack themselves.
    a. reciprocity variable
    b. maintenance hypothesis
    c. sensitivity variable
    d. complementary hypothesis

18. Ordinary-looking women were judged to be _____ when seen in the company of very attractive-looking women than when seen with unattractive or other ordinary-looking women.
    a. foolish for competing with very attractive women
    b. forgettable
    c. more attractive
    d. less attractive

19. _____ are seen as less secure, less mature, and more self-absorbed.
    a. males
    b. females
    c. early disclosers
    d. late disclosers

20. At which stage in Levinger's development stages of a relationship would "we-ness" occur?
    a. mutuality
    b. self-disclosure
    c. deep contact
    d. bonding

21. A need for _____ refers to a need for very close, personal, and meaningful interaction with another person on a physical, emotional, and/or intellectual level.
    a. sex
    b. intimacy
    c. marriage
    d. dependence

70 YOUR WORLDS

PEOPLE: HOW MUCH DO YOU KNOW?

Write what you can about the people listed below (as it relates to what you learned in this chapter).

Kobasa

Levinger

relationships move thru 4 predictable stages
(1) Zero contact 2) awareness (3) surface contact (4) mutuality

Schachter

Ordinal Position Hypothesis

PERSONAL GROWTH EXERCISE - FRIENDSHIP

<u>PURPOSE</u> To gain insight into your friendships.

1. What qualities do you value in a friend?

2. What qualities do you posses to offer a friend?

3. What qualities do you lack which you would like to have?

4. Can you think of any ways to develop those qualities and/or to become a better friend?

PERSONAL GROWTH EXERCISE - SELF-DISCLOSURE

PURPOSE   To discover your own level of disclosure in relationships which are important to you.

Everyone has relationships that don't work out (you wanted to join the "in" clique at school or the sorority/fraternity at college; you wanted to get to know someone better, but they were not interested in you; you had a good friend who let you down in some way, or whom you disappointed; you are estranged from a parent or relative; you are no longer involved with a member of the opposite sex whom you once loved, or still love)

1. In which of the stages described by Levinger did the relationship(s) fall apart?

   Stage 1, Zero Contact -

   Stage 2, Awareness -

   Stage 3, Surface Contact -

   Stage 4, Mutuality -

2. Do you feel that more information about and/or care in the Stage 3 could have saved the relationship(s)? (To review: this is the stage where people explore similarities and reciprocity; initially by engaging in small talk and later in self-disclosure.)

3. Are you an early discloser, a late discloser, or a non-discloser?

4. Do you feel this helps or hurts your relationships?

5. Can you think of ways to change your pattern of disclosure so that you either wait until it is more appropriate to disclose personal information about yourself (if you are an early discloser), or so that you can learn to trust others enough to open up more (if you are a non-discloser)?

PERSONAL GROWTH EXERCISE - FRIENDSHIPS

PURPOSE To understand the influences that other people have had on your life.

1. Think back to when you were very young. Do you feel that you had an excellent, good, acceptable, or poor relationship with your primary caregiver? (Most teenagers go through a few rough spots with their parents so do not allow this to distort your perception!) What positive and/or negative qualities/characteristics do you remember?

2. Think back to when you were in grade school. What types of friendships did you have? What were your expectations of your friends? What were their expectations of you? Are any of these friends still an important part of your life? Why, or why not?

3. Repeat the above exercise, but using high school friendships.

4. What influences do you feel these relationships have had on the kind of person you are today?

CHAPTER 7

Your Intimate World: Sex and Sexual Relationships

LEARNING OBJECTIVES

1. To understand male and female sexual anatomy and functioning.
2. Analyze the current and the historical attitudes toward sex in this country.
3. Recognize the need for sexual adjustment in long-term relationships, with age, and when confronted with special sexual problems.

CHAPTER OUTLINE

I. SEXUAL ANATOMY, SEXUAL FUNCTIONING, AND SEXUAL BEHAVIOR
   A. Sexual Anatomy and Functioning
      1. Androgens: male hormones, begin production in the testes about 8 weeks after conception
         a. Testosterone: promotes development of male sex organs and represses development of female sex organs (the most important male hormone). Increased production in puberty resulting in dramatic changes:
            i. enlarged testes and penis
            ii. growth of facial and body hair
            iii. growth spurts (2 years behind females but continues for 2 years longer)
            iv. voice deepens
         b. Penis: the male sex organ that transmits sperm to the female during intercourse
         c. Testes: produce sperm
         d. Scrotum: sac which contains the testes, and hangs away from the body in order to maintain an even temperature for potency of the sperm
         e. Urethra: sperm travel through special ducts and canals

76   YOUR WORLDS

                    into the urethra and from here are ejaculated during
                    male organism (urine is also carried via the urethra,
                    but a special valve prevents mixing of the urine with
                    the sperm)
                f. Estrogens: female hormones which determine the ability
                    to become pregnant
                g. Ovaries: produce the hormones and the egg (ova)
                h. Vagina: a tube-like cavity, 3-5 inches long which re-
                    ceives the male penis during intercourse and serves as
                    the exit canal for a baby
                i. Cervix: connects the vagina and the uterus
                j. Uterus: connected to the female ovaries by means of:
                k. Fallopian tubes: which carry the eggs to the uterus
                    where fertilization takes place
                l. Female organism: female sexual pleasure is only nomi-
                    nally related to the reproductive process. Some people
                    argue that organism results from vaginal stimulation
                    by the penis, however, it is the stimulation of the
                    clitoris which plays a central role
                m. Clitoris: a small external organ which, like the penis,
                    becomes engorged with blood and enlarged during sexual
                    stimulation
                n. Both males and females produce both male and female
                    hormones
        B. Sexual Behavior
            1. Terms (See Exhibit 7-1 in your text)
                a. Anal sex
                b. Coitus
                c. Cunnilingus
                d. Ejaculation
                e. Fellacio
                f. Foreplay
                g. Masturbation
                h. Oral sex
                i. Organism
                j. Petting
                k. Refractory period
                l. Sex tension flush
            2. Oral sex (fellatio and cunnilingus): may be part of heavy
                petting or the foreplay for coitus. Practice is somewhat
                more common among the college-educated
            3. Anal sex: common among male homosexuals and a small percen-
                tage of heterosexual couples
            4. Masturbation: self-stimulation
        C. The Sexual Response Cycle (Masters and Johnson):
            1. Physiological responses to the sexual experience
            2. Stage 1: Excitement Phase:
                a. Increases in heart rate, blood pressure, breathing
                b. Nipples become erect, clitoris expands, the inner
                    vagina lengthens and is lubricated
                c. Blood rushes to the penis, which becomes erect

YOUR INTIMATE WORLD: SEX AND SEXUAL RELATIONSHIPS

        d. Sex tension flush may be experienced by either sex but is more common in females
        e. Behavioral precursers: kissing, petting etc
        f. Cognitive precursers: explicit sex talk, fantasizing, (stimulation occurs in the mind and is tranferred to the body)
    3. Stage 2: Plateau Phase
        a. Early physical responses intensify
        b. Sometimes the penis secretes fluid containing sperm and even if full penetration and ejaculation does not take place the female could still become pregnant
        c. Penis may become dark in color
        d. Female breasts may enlarge
    4. Stage 3: Orgasmic Phase
        a. Involuntary muscle contractions in the pelvic region (males and females) 5 every 4 seconds for 30 seconds
        b. For males: involuntary ejaculation (about 1 teaspoon)
        c. Awareness narrows to a purely physical level
        d. Females reach this phase much later than males
    5. State 4: Resolution Phase
        a. Physiological functioning returns to normal
        b. Refractory period - varies from male to male but increases with age
        c. Women do not experience a refractory period and may experience multiple organisms
D. Myths About Orgasms (see Exhibit 7-2 in your text)
E. Choice of a Sex Partner: Heterosexuality or Homosexuality
    1. Heterosexuals: the sexual partner is a member of the opposite sex
        a. Males: 75-80% exclusively heterosexual
        b. Females: 85-90% exclusively heterosexual
    2. Homosexuality: 2% of males, 1% of females exclusively attracted to same-sex partners
    3. Bi-sexual: attracted to and engage in sex with members of both sexes. Estimated 25 million in the U.S. have experienced both heterosexual and homosexual experiences
    4. Homosexual preferences (speculative)
        a. Genetic predisposition
        b. Patterns of upbringing
        c. Reinforced homosexual experiences in adolescence
        d. Not a mental disorder
        e. Homosexuals do not feel a need to be "cured"
        f. Social stigma still exists
    5. A.I.D.S. (Acquired Immune Difficiency Syndrome)
        a. Has undermined the breakdown of the social stigma attached to homesexuality
        b. Homophobia has returned (an exaggerated fear of homosexuals)
        c. Not simply a "gay disease"
        d. Africa - origin of the virus, has widespread heterosexual A.I.D.S. population

78 YOUR WORLDS

        e. Casual contact does not spread A.I.D.S.

II. ATTITUDES TOWARD SEX
    A. The Need for Physical Closeness
       1. Touching, hugging, kissing, patting, sexual intercourse
       2. Need for intimacy
       3. Physiological release
       4. Procreation: historically prevailing attitude
       5. Recreation: a relatively new idea
    B. Behind the Revolution (in the 1960s)
       1. The birth control pill
       2. Reduced parental supervision
       3. Access to automobiles
       4. Relaxed supervision at colleges
    C. Increased sexual activity led to:
       1. Reduced fears of unwanted pregnancy
       2. Sex as a natural part of dating
       3. Commercialization of sex
       4. Pressure to engage in sexual activity
       5. Mythical sexual standards
    D. Where Do We Go From Here?
       1. The majority of males and females will engage in premarital sex
       2. Extramarital affairs will not rise significantly (upper limit - 50%)
       3. The "affection rider" will remain important in sexual relationships
       4. Rates of casual sex will dimished due to:
          a. Disillusionment with uncommitted encounters
          b. Trend toward conservative values in society
          c. Fears of sexually transmitted diseases
    E. Note: Much of the data on sexual behavior and attitudes is based on questionnaire responses and, therefore, has to be interpreted with caution

III. SEXUAL ADJUSTMENT IN LONG-TERM RELATIONSHIPS
    A. Unequal Desire for Sexual Activity
       1. Alfred Kinsey Report on Sexual Behavior:
          a. 6,000 interviews
          b. Married couples in their 20s and 30s reported having sexual intercourse once or twice a week
          c. Other couples felt a "standard" had been set for the rate of sexual intercourse in marriage after hearing the results of the study
       2. Traditionally the male desired more sexual activity
       3. Recently, the female complains about husbands who do not make love often enough
       4. Reasons for reduced sexual urge: stress at work, career demands, demands of childbearing and rearing, illness or

YOUR INTIMATE WORLD: SEX AND SEXUAL RELATIONSHIPS

drugs, anxiety, hostility, anger, depression, and/or problems with the relationship
5. Ebb and flow of desire is normal in a long-term relationship
6. Persistent inequality of desire for sex can create serious problems - frustration and anger, guilt and pressure - and could lead to affairs or divorce
7. Communication is vital for solving the problem and for maintaining intimacy while it persists

B. Boredom
 1. Predictability of the sexual experience
 2. Solution: try variety in how not who
 3. Erotic materials can stimulate interest, but its use is controversial:
    a. Attorney General Edwin Meese's Commission on Pornography (not a scientific study) found a causal link between erotica of a violent nature and aggression toward women; material that degrades women and sexual violence; no erotica is harmless
    b. The President's Commission on Obscenity and Pornography concluded that sexually explicit material was NOT a significant cause of sexual violence and abuse
    c. Pornography: erotic material with no socially redeeming value (a subjective opinion)
    e. Social scientists agree that violence is the key to abusive behavior not the sex
    f. Recommendations from the Meese panel: increase laws to restrict pornography and give longer jail sentences to violators

C. Extradyadic Relationships: sexual relationship(s) outside a steady, cohabiting, or marriage relationship
 1. <u>Open Marriage</u> (authors, the O"Neills): this 1972 book proposed that couples should allow other opposite-sex relationships (sexual and otherwise). Mutual participation is critical
 2. Swinging: involves both partners in controlled extradyadic sex with no emotional ties

D. Sexual Adjustment With Age
 1. Sexual desire does not disappear with age
 2. Males take longer and require more stimulation to achieve an erection
 3. Womens' vaginas become less elastic and lubrication decreases
 4. Orgasms tend to be less intense
 5. Frequency of sexual intercourse decreases with time
 6. Most couples in their 70s still make love

E. Special Sexual Problems
 1. Sexually transmitted diseases STDs): syphillis, gonorrhea, herpes, chlamydia, HPV, AIDS
    a. 27,000 new cases of STDs are reported <u>daily</u>
    b. See Table 7-1 in your text for symptoms

2. Behaviors that put you at risk:
    a. Sharing drug needles and syringes
    b. Anal sex with or without a condom
    c. Vaginal sex with someone who uses drugs or engages in anal sex
    d. Sex with someone you don't know very well
    e. Sex with someone who has had many sexual partners
    f. Sex with someone exhibiting symptoms of an STD
3. Engage in "safe sex" and "responsible sexual behavior"

F. Sexual Dysfunctions
1. Masters and Johnson believe that most difficulties arise due to attitudes, fears and inhibitions regarding sex:
    a. Sex is dirty
    b. Deviations are shameful
    c. Sexual inadequacy: created by the new sexual freedom
2. Common male sexual dysfunctions (see Exhibit 7-3 in your text for definitions)
    a. Erectile dysfunction
    b. Premature ejaculation
    c. Retarded ejaculation
3. Common female sexual dysfunctions
    a. Vaginismus
    b. Dyspareunia
    c. Orgasmic dysfunction
    d. Female sexual arousal disorder (primary or secondary)
4. Other reasons for sexual dysfunctions:
    a. Poor relationship
    b. Inconsiderate partner
    c. Lack of skill of sexual partner
    d. Past negative experiences with sex
    e. Rape
    f. Medication
5. Treatment
    a. Rule out a medical problem by having a physical
    b. Seek professional help as a couple

G. Unwanted Pregnancy: due to carelessness, ignorance, and/or lack of responsibility (see Table 7-2 in your text for methods of birth control)
1. "Baby roulette" - leaving the consequences of sex to fate
2. One partner wants a baby and believes the other will be won over once the deed is done
3. Preventing an unwanted pregnancy is _your_ responsibility
4. What to do?
    a. Have the baby and raise it
    b. Have the baby and give it up for adoption
    c. Terminate the pregnancy

H. Sexual Liability: courtroom battles over sexual issues

REVIEW QUESTIONS

YOUR INTIMATE WORLD: SEX AND SEXUAL RELATIONSHIPS 81

MATCHING: Match the words and phrases below with the definitions

a. pornography
b. androgens
c. estrogens
d. excitement phase of sexual response cycle
e. plateau phase of sexual response cycle
f. resolution phase of sexual response cycle
g. swinging
h. reorientation therapy
i. orgasmic phase of sexual response cycle
j. extradyadic relationship

1. _b_ Male hormones produced in the testes starting about 8 weeks after conception.
2. _c_ Female hormones which are produced by the ovaries.
3. _d_ The phase in which the heart rate, blood pressure and breathing rate increase.
4. _e_ The second phase of Masters and Johnson's model.
5. _i_ Characterized by involuntary muscle contractions.
6. _f_ When males will experience a refractory period.
7. _h_ Available for homosexuals who wish to change their sexual preferences.
8. _j_ A sexual encounter or relationship outside a steady, cohabiting, or marriage relationship.
9. _a_ Erotic material with no socially redeeming value.
10. _g_ Sex without emotional involvement.

PEOPLE YOU SHOULD KNOW

Kinsey
Meese
O'Neills
Masters and Johnson

FILL-IN QUESTIONS

1. The _sex drive_ is a basic biological urge; our bodies are programmed for it to enable us to reproduce ourselves.
2. Male hormones are called _androgens_. The most important of which is _testosterone_
3. Female hormones are called _estrogen_ and are produced by the _ovaries_.
4. _cunnilingus_ and _fellatio_ are forms of oral sex.
5. _refractory period_ is the time following ejaculation during which the male is unable to experience another orgasm.
6. The four stage model of human sexual response includes: _excitement_ phase, _plateau_ phase, _orgasm_ phase, and the _resolution_ phase.

82 YOUR WORLDS

7. A major factor in the sexual revolution was the _pill_.
8. _swinging_ involves both partners in controlled extradyadic sex.
9. In 1984 there were _25,000_ new cases of one or another STDs reported _daily_.
10. Weight-loss, tiredness, fever, swollen glands, diarrhea, and loss of appetite are all symptoms of _AIDS_.

TRUE-FALSE QUESTIONS

T (F) 1. The problems of human sexuality have been solved/reduced now that they are out in the open and may be discussed freely, and now that people are able to pursue sex without the old restraints and taboos.

T (F) 2. Males and females grow at the same time and the same rate during puberty.

(T) F 3. Male hormones are produced in the testes about eight weeks after conception.

T (F) 4. Estrogens are produced in the fallopian tubes.

(T) F 5. Masturbation is a common practice among married and unmarried members of both sexes.

(T) F 6. Masters and Johnson moved the study of human sexual experience into the realm of science by observing sexual activity directly.

T (F) 7. A sex tension flush may only be experienced by women.

(T) F 8. It is possible for a woman to become pregnant during heavy petting even though full penetration does not occur.

T (F) 9. A male often experiences orgasm during the refractory period.

T (F) 10. Coitus without orgasm is harmful to males.

(T) F 11. Data suggests that 25 million American adults have had both heterosexual and homosexual experiences.

T (F) 12. There is evidence that most homosexuals would like to be "cured."

(T) F 13. Attitudes toward sex are influenced significantly by the values of a particular culture.

T (F) 14. A.I.D.S. is a "gay disease."

YOUR INTIMATE WORLD: SEX AND SEXUAL RELATIONSHIPS   83

15. Sex, as an enjoyable recreational activity for members of both sexes is a relatively new idea.

16. Attitudes toward infidelity remain basically negative.

17. Both men and women believe that strong affection should play an important role in sexual relationships.

18. In the latest large-scale survey, the most frequent complaint women had about sex was that they did not reach orgasm often enough.

19. The frequency of sexual intercourse between couples drops off with almost every passing year.

20. Sexually transmitted diseases are being controlled successfully in this country today (excluding A.I.D.S.).

MULTIPLE-CHOICE QUESTIONS

1. Your transition from child to adult capable of reproducing the species was a(n) _____ event of great significance.
    a. adolescent
    b. educational
    c. cultural
    d. biological

2. The most important male hormone is called:
    a. endrogen
    b. estorgen
    c. testosterone
    d. progesterone

3. A tube-like cavity, normally 3-5 inches in length which expands during intercourse.
    a. penis
    b. testes
    c. scrotum
    d. vagina

4. Which part of the female anatomy appears to play the central role in female sexual stimulation?
    a. penis
    b. clitoris
    c. vagina
    d. mind

5. A sexual practice which is a common practice among married and unmarried members of both sexes.
    a. fellatio
    b. masturbation

84 YOUR WORLDS

       c. cunnilingus
       d. anal sex

6. Masters and Johnson proposed:
    a. banning sexually explicit materials
    b. open marriage
    c. strictor laws preventing pornography
    d. the model of the sexual response cycle

7. The _____ phase of the sexual reponse cycle is when physiological functioning returns to normal - a cooling-down period.
    a. orgasmic
    b. resolution
    c. refractory
    d. plateau

8. Research has confirmed that women typically:
    a. take four times as long as men to reach orgasm
    b. take three times as long as men to reach orgasm
    c. take twice as long as men to reach orgasm
    d. reach orgasm at the same time as men

9. It has been estimated that what percent of the male population is exclusively heterosexual?
    a. 75-80
    b. 80-85
    c. 85-90
    d. 90-95

10. Homosexuality was once considered to be:
    a. illegal
    b. sinful
    c. a mental disorder
    d. all of the above

11. It is feared that A.I.D.S. will undermine the social progress toward acceptance of homosexuals and bring about a return to:
    a. homophobia
    b. hemophillia
    c. homophillia
    d. hemophobia

12. New attitudes toward sex have led to:
    a. increased pressures for many
    b. decreased pressures for everyone
    c. total freedom for everyone who wants it
    d. increased honesty about sex

13. What is happening to the gap between the number of men and the number of women who admit to having extramarital sexual encounters?
    a. it is increasing

(b.) it is narrowing
   c. the same
   d. it is marginal

14. There is evidence that the incidence of casual sex:
    (a.) will diminish
    b. will increase
    c. will decrease for women only
    d. will increase for women only

15. Which of the following is NOT a problem detailed in your text that many couples face at one time or another?
    a. unequal sexual desire
    b. boredom
    (c.) extradyadic relationships
    d. aging

16. Who published a major report on the subect of sexual behavior after interviewing more than 6,000 people?
    a. the O'Neills
    b. Edwin Meese
    c. Masters and Johnson
    (d.) Alfred Kinsey

17. A controversial method of combatting boredom in a sexual relationship was mentioned in your text. What was it?
    a. reorientation therapy
    b. sex therapy
    c. confrontation
    (d.) the use of erotic materials

18. In all relationships, sexual activity is affected by:
    a. age
    b. the relationship
    (c.) age and the age of the relationship
    d. heredity

19. In 1984, there were 27,000 new cases of one or another of the STDs reported:
    (a.) every day
    b. every week
    c. every month
    d. for that year

20. What is the term used to describe a sexual functioning difficulty that has physical symptoms?
    a. physiological dysfunction
    (b.) sexual dysfunction
    c. orgasmic problems
    d. orgasmic dysfunction

86 YOUR WORLDS

PEOPLE: HOW MUCH DO YOU KNOW?

Write what you can about the people listed below (as it relates to what you learned in this chapter).

Kinsey

Meese

O'Neills

Masters and Johnson

YOUR INTIMATE WORLD: SEX AND SEXUAL RELATIONSHIPS

PERSONAL GROWTH EXERCISE - YOUR SEXUALITY

<u>PURPOSE</u>   To explore your knowledge of your own sexuality, and to suggest ways to prevent boredom in long-term sexual relationships.

1. Are you now or have you ever been involved in a sexual relationship?

    Yes _____   No _____

2. What is important to you in a sexual partner?

3. Do you know what turns you on physically?   Yes _____   No _____

    List the things that you enjoy:

4. Does your partner know what turns you on?   Yes _____   No _____

    List the things your partner thinks you enjoy:

5. Do you know what turns your partner on?   Yes _____   No _____

    List the things you think your partner enjoys:

6. Do you ever feel frustrated by something your partner does, or does not do, sexually?
    Yes _____   No _____

7. If yes, have you ever told your partner how you feel about this?
    Yes _____   No _____

8. Do you feel embarrassed talking about your sexual needs or the needs of your partner?
    Yes _____   No _____

9. Do you feel that your partner should know how to make love to you without any suggestions from you?   Yes _____   No _____

10. Your text describes how sexual boredom can affect a relationship. If you are married or engaged in a long-term sexual relationship which is either not altogether sexually satisfying, or has become stuck in a boring routine sexually, try fantasy coupon swapping with your mate in order to put more spice into your relationship.

    Each of you should write several sexual activities onto 3 x 5 cards. These should be things which you enjoy doing or would like to try for the first time. They could range from going out for a romantic meal, spending at least 10-15 minutes kissing prior to other sexual activity, greeting your partner at the front door in an exotic costume, engaging in oral sex, etc. to getting someone to keep the children overnight (if you have children). Try to avoid things which would require a large budget (for example, a romantic trip to the Bahamas would be nice, but impractical for most people!). Try to avoid things which you know would upset your partner, but at the same time each of you must avoid bringing any pre-conceived ideas to this exercise (I will hate this; this is a waste of time; who did you do this with before me; isn't our relationship good enough for you; etc.).

    Next, agree on a time schedule - once a week or once a month would be a good way to start.

    Now exchange one card each per time schedule.

    The agreement between you is that at some time during the agreed upon time period you will arrange for the coupon's wish to be carried out. The receiver of the card decides exactly when this will occur, and the person who gave the card must comply at that time.

    <u>Never</u> use this technique vindictively.

PERSONAL GROWTH EXERCISE - SEXUAL STEREOTYPES

PURPOSE To discover how much you allow the commercialized ideals of sex and sex partners to affect your life.

Are you taken in by the "shoulds" of sex?

1. If I'm dating someone we should make love.

2. I should date someone who is slim and goodlooking.

3. I will never get married unless I lose weight.

4. We should make love 2-3 times a week or else we are not normal. (married couples or those living together)

5. I should become aroused by my mate as soon as he/she attempts to turn me on.

6. I should be able to handle a career, spouse, and children without anything or anyone suffering from neglect.

7. If I really love him/her and he/she really loves me then making love will be perfect every time.

8. Every time we make love I should feel the earth move.

9. Any married couple that hasn't made love for three weeks is in real trouble.

10. Unless we make love in a different position each time our marriage will become boring and fail.

Can you think of any other "shoulds" which either you or someone you know has allowed to control your/their life?

CHAPTER 8
Your Special Relationships: Love and Marraige

LEARNING OBJECTIVES

1. To understand that love is not purely and simply an emotion which is easily described and understood.

2. Detail the many different reasons for marriage, both historically and in America today.

3. To comprehend the many different kinds of adjustments everyone must be expected to make when they make a total commitment to marriage, and to learn ways to make these adjustments successfully.

CHAPTER OUTLINE

I. LOVE
    A. What is Love?
       1. Storge: love shared by parents and children
       2. Philla: the deepest friendship
       3. Agape: selfless humanitarian love
       4. Eros: romantic love
       5. Humanist's view of love:
          a. Part of the fulfillment of human potential
          b. The expression of a healthy personality
       6. Psychoanylic view of love:
          a. Emphasizes drives and needs (primarily sexual)
          b. Love is a condition for developing a healthy personality
       7. Cognitive view of love:
          a. Emphasizes the role thinking plays in being in love
          b. Certain beliefs are held
          c. Self-deception may be necessary (love is blind)

8. Behavioral view of love:
   a. Conditioned responses are generalized and applied to a particular person
   b. Behaviors and responses are learned long before we fall in love
9. Feelings associated with Love include: happiness, joy, peace, fulfillment, ecstasy, misery, uncertainty, pain, jealousy, depression and hate

B. A Triangular Theory of Love
   1. Conclusions based on a survey by Sternberg
   2. Identifying the nature of love
   3. Best understood in terms of a set of separate aspects:
      a. Valuing the loved one in one's life
      b. Promoting the welfare of the loved one
      c. Sharing oneself and one's things
      d. Being able to count on the loved one in times of need
   4. These aspects fit any kind of love relationship and may be grouped under the three sides of the triangle which are:
      a. Passion: the motivational component
      b. Commitment: the cognitive component (short or long-term)
      c. Intimacy: the emotional component
   5. Different love relationships are visualized as triangles of different shapes depending on which of the three components are most important in the relationship:
      a. Parent/child: commitment is strongest, therefore has the longest line
      b. Best friend: intimacy is strongest
      c. Infatuation: passion is strongest
   6. In all Sternberg described eight possible kinds of love relationships
   7. Further research into romantic love relationships examined how the perceptions couples have of their own triangle affects satisfaction with the relationship
      a. A match between how a person would like the other person in the relationship to feel about him/her and how they perceive the other person feels is critical
      b. The perception does not necessarily have to be correct
      c. Communication about one's feelings, therefore, is vital
   8. This theory allows specific research questions about love to be tested in a scientific manner

C. How Do You Know If You Are In Love?
   1. Walster and Walster define three conditions that must be true for a person to "fall in love"
      a. The culture must promote the ideal of romantic love
      b. The "right person" comes along
      c. A physiological arousal occurs which is interpreted as love
   2. Factors that influence labeling:
      a. How long the feeling lasts
      b. Your own attitudes and values (one may label a strong physical attraction as love or as lust)

YOUR SPECIAL RELATIONSHIPS: LOVE AND MARRIAGE

        3. There is no objective standard for being in love
- D. Romantic Love in Perspective
    1. The most popular theme for books, songs, movies and plays
    2. Passionate, romantic love seldom lasts
    3. Companionate love replaces romantic love:
        a. Characterized by trust, respect, appreciation, loyalty and support as well as by heightened emotion
        b. Based on accepting a person as they really are (not as idealized) and caring beyond physical attraction
        c. Personal characteristics which make it easier to love and maintain a successful love relationship include: good self-esteem, the ability to meet one's own basic needs, contact with reality, the ability to deal with frustration, reasonable expectations
        d. The above characteristics are similar to those needed for any friendship and for effective behavior in any situation
        e. Companionate love versus friendship has: higher levels of exclusiveness, fascination, and sexual desire; a greater depth of caring; greater capacity for strongly positive emotional experience; greater potential for conflict, ambivalence, mutual criticism, and distress

II. MARRIAGE
- A. Changes:
    1. People are marrying later
    2. People are marrying more often
    3. Divorce:
        a. Increasing again after a 2-year decline
        b. Divorced people usually remarry within 5 years (75% of females and 80% of males)
    4. Cohabitation without marriage is increasing
    5. Choosing to remain single is more acceptable today
- B. Why Do We Marry?
    1. Love: 56% of females and 36% of males gave this as their primary reason in a 1979 survey
    2. Companionship: mutual and realistic expectations necessary
    3. Children: society still feels marriage is appropriate for practical as well as moral reasons
    4. Other reasons include: financial security, because marriage is expected, and to escape a situation
- C. Satisfaction With Marriage
    1. Most married people report being more satisfied with their lives than single, divorced, or widowed people
    2. Married women are less satisfied on all criteria than men
    3. Psychological distrubances are higher for married women than for single women, but the opposite is true for married versus single men
- D. Increasing the Chances for Marital Satisfaction and Success
    1. Age: divorce rates are higher for couples who marry in

their teens or wait until their late 20s or after
2. Commitment: a desire to get and to be married
3. Emotional health: the ability to get along fine on your own
4. Family history: parents had a satisfactory marriage
5. Financial status: lack of money creates pressures
6. Similar backgrounds
7. Realistic expectations: about fidelity, children, life-style, etc.
8. Open communication and honesty increase trust
9. Satisfactory sexual relationship: more frequent sexual intercourse and marital happiness appear to go together

E. Trial Marriages
 1. Definition of trial marriage: cohabitation prior to a commitment to marriage
 2. Statistics show that for those who engage in a trial marriage:
   a. Divorce rates are at least as great
   b. Satisfaction with marriage is significantly lower
   c. Expectations for marriage are higher
   d. Commitment to being married may be lower, however the expectations to get married may be higher
 3. Psychologists do not have much data on the dynamics of cohabitation and there are still many questions to be answered

F. Adjusting to Marriage
 1. Life-style adjustments: reaching mutually agreeable decisions:
   a. Taking out the garbage
   b. Where you will live
   c. What car you will buy
   d. Will you share household chores
   e. These decisions used to be easier when traditional marriages were the norm
 2. Mutual expectations are, again, critical, and should be discussed prior to marriage. Don't assume anything and don't expect miraculous changes after the wedding bells
 3. Compromises are easier before it is a win-lose issue
 4. Pre-nuptual agreements (marriage contracts)
   a. Keeps financial assets separate
   b. Specifies rights and obligations of each spouse
   c. How children will be raised
   d. Conditions for terminating the marriage
   e. Few young couples getting married for the first time make contracts
   f. Rates are slightly higher for older individuals with considerable financial assets or with children from previous marriages to protect
 5. Financial Adjustments
   a. Couples argue more about money than anything else
   b. "Money" is also about security, power, and values
   c. Important: set mutually agreed upon priorities and

           goals
       d. Decide who will manage the money
       e. Keep arguments about money about money only
    6. Adjusting to children
       a. Parents have less freedom and less time together
       b. Primary caregiver is often overtired
       c. Financial needs increase
       d. Jealousy often occurs
       e. Arguments about child rearing occur
       f. Marital satisfaction often declines when **children** are born and remains low until they are grown
       g. Important: self-esteem for husband/new father and satisfaction with her role in the marriage for wife/new mother
       h. More couples are choosing to remain childless
       i. More singles are choosing to adopt children
       j. Parents are much more involved in their children's lives today (intellectual, social, emotional, and academic) as compared to 1950s parents who saw themselves as providers, caretakers and disciplinarians
       k. Family size: limited to one or two children
       l. Working mothers: 50% with children under 6 and 64% with children over 6
       m. "The typical American family" no longer a majority but "the family" is alive and well
    7. Adjusting to Marital Discord
       a. The perfect marriage does not exist
       b. Arguments will occur and couples should begin early to find ways to keep discord within bounds:
           i. get it out in the open, don't brood
           ii. state the problem you are having, don't accuse
           iii. stick to the subject and to the present
           iv. don't go to sleep angry with each other
           v. fight fairly
G. Types of Marriage (Cuber and Harrof)
    1. Conflict habituated: arguing has become a way of life
    2. Devitalized: boredom has set in, and partners don't even argue anymore
    3. Passive-congenial: no conflict because partners don't put energy into the relationship, their interests lie elsewhere (careers, children)
    4. Total: a vital marriage with a more complete sharing and emotional closeness, partners make a point of spending lots of time together
    5. Vital: the marriage is important to both and the partners try to work things out
    6. Most marriages fall into the first three catagories, but the couples are relatively content. These are simply the adjustments they chose to make

96 YOUR WORLDS

REVIEW QUESTIONS

MATCHING: Match the words and phrases below with the definitions

a. behavioral view of love
b. trial marriage
c. intimacy
d. marital discord
e. cognitive view of love
f. cohabitation
g. psychoanalytic view of love
h. prenuptial agreement
i. humanist view of love
j. triangular theory of love

1. _a_ Love is based on a set of conditioned responses that have been generalized and then applied to a particular person.
2. _g_ Emphasizes the role of drives and needs in love.
3. _e_ Emphasizes the role that thinking plays in being in love.
4. _i_ Sees the capacity to love and be loved as part of the fulfillment of human potential.
5. _j_ Contains the elements of passion, commitment, and intimacy.
6. _c_ The emotional component.
7. _b_ Cohabitation prior to the commitment for marriage.
8. _f_ Living together.
9. _h_ A marriage contract.
10. _d_ A source of great distress to many people, but an inevitable factor in all marriages

PEOPLE YOU SHOULD KNOW

Sternberg — *tri theory of love*   Cuber and Harrof — *types of marriages*
Walster and Walster — *conditioning of love*   Harlow

FILL-IN QUESTIONS

1. According to the _Behavioral_ view, love is based on a set of conditioned responses.

2. In the _humanistic_ view, a good love relationship is the expression of a healthy personality.

3. Sternberg developed the _triangular theory of love_ when he tried to diffentiate romantic love from infatuation and companionate love or parent/child love.

4. People who are _romantic by nature_ are more likely to call physical arousal by the name of love than those who are not.

5. In love, as in most things, if you expect _perfection_ you are likely to be disappointed.

6. Women today tend to postpone mariage until sometime between _23_ and _24_ and men until _26_.

YOUR SPECIAL RELATIONSHIPS: LOVE AND MARRIAGE   97

7. Today most people in this country marry for _love_.
8. The reason most people give for choosing to remain single is _personal freedom_.
9. Cohabitation prior to commitment to marriage is known as _trial marriage_.
10. Deciding upon who takes out the garbage and/or who does the dishes would be referred to as a _life style adjustment_.
11. A contract which would decide on property division and alimony prior to marriage would be called a _prenuptial agreement_.
12. A golden rule is to "keep arguments about money _about money_."

TRUE-FALSE QUESTIONS

T (F) 1. Philla is a selfless humanitarian love.

(T) F 2. According to the behavioral view, love is based on a set of conditioned responses that have been generalized to a particular person.

T (F) 3. Sternberg's Triangular Theory of Love is a model which describes romantic love relationships between three people (the "other woman" or man).

(T) F 4. According to Sternberg, in an infatuation relationship passion is the dominating compenent, intimacy is moderate, and commitment is missing.

(T) F 5. For most people the difference between love and infatuation is evident only after some period of time.

T (F) 6. For a successful long-term relationship, people should look for a partner who will meet their own basic needs and whose basic needs they can meet.

(T) F 7. There is evidence that the same personal characteristics which lead to effective behavior also make people more accepting and appreciative of love and friendship.

T (F) 8. It is rarely possible for two people who are very good friends to make a success of falling in love.

(T) F 9. When comparing <u>love relationships</u> to friendships, it has been found that the former has greater potential for conflict, ambivalence, mutual criticism, and distress.

T (F) 10. A recent survey of college undergraduate women shows that most of these women intend to marry as soon as they graduate but

98 YOUR WORLDS

               will delay having children until they are established in their careers.

(T) F 11. The divorce rate in this country is climbing again, but statistics show that most divorced people will remarry within five years.

T (F) 12. Most divorces occur in the eighth year of marriage (following the "7-year itch").

(T) F 13. Single people are sometimes paid less for comparable work than married people because they have no family to support.

(T) F 14. The estimated cost of raising a child from birth through four years of college is over $200,000.

(T) F 15. No matter how it is measured, nor what it is called (satisfaction, happiness, adjustment, etc.), women long have had a less favorable response to marriage than men.

T (F) 16. A study of over 300 couples found that satisfaction with marriage was significantly higher for couples who had cohabited prior to marriage than those who had not.

T (F) 17. Single men are rarely allowed to adopt a child and single women do not have much success with adoption either.

T (F) 18. Arguments occur in a marriage only when the marriage is heading for trouble or is already in trouble.

MULTIPLE-CHOICE QUESTIONS

1. The well-known psychologist Harry Harlow stated, in 1958, that psychologists know less about love than:
    a. psychiatrists
    b. psychoanalysts
    c. marriage counselors
    (d.) poets and novelists

2. What was the name that the ancient Greeks gave to the love between a parent and child?
    (a.) storge
    b. philla
    c. eros
    d. agape

3. Which theorists would view love as something which is based on drives and needs?
    a. humanist
    (b.) psychoanalytic

c. cognitive
d. behavioral

5. Which of the following is NOT a feeling reported by people who are in love?
   a. joy
   b. peace
   c. hate
   d. all are ligitimate feelings

6. The motivational component in Sternberg's Triangle Theory of Love is:
   a. commitment
   b. passion
   c. intimacy
   d. infatuation

7. What is the component in Sternberg's theory which includes support, communication, and sharing?
   a. commitment
   b. passion
   c. intimacy
   d. infatuation

8. In a parent-child relationship in Sternberg's model the longest line would be representing which compenent?
   a. commitment
   b. passion
   c. intimacy
   d. infatuation

9. Studies have shown that what is important for satisfaction in a romantic relationship is:
   a. the way your partner feels about you
   b. the way you feel about your partner
   c. the way you believe your partner feels about you
   d. the way relatives and friends perceive you as a couple

10. Which of the following is NOT defined by Walster and Walster as a condition necessary for a person to "fall in love?"
    a. the culture must promote the ideal of romantic love
    b. the right person must come along
    c. physiological arousal must be interpreted as love
    d. an exchange of intimate communication with the loved one

11. Psychologists agree that people who are _____ by nature are more likely to give the feeling of physical attraction the name of love rather than of lust.
    a. religious
    b. romantic
    c. humanistic

d. passionate

12. Which type of love is characterized by trust, respect, appreciation, loyalty, and support as well as by heightened emotion.
    a. companionate
    b. romantic
    c. passionate
    d. modern

13. People with _____ are more likely to be looking to be loved than to love another.
    a. unreasonable expectations
    b. several children
    c. low self-esteem
    d. no commitment

14. Most divorced people will remarry within how many years of their divorce?
    a. two years
    b. three years
    c. five years
    d. eight years

15. In a national survey a few years ago it was found that 56% of the women and 39% of the men married:
    a. for financial reasons
    b. to have children
    c. for companionship
    d. for love

16. Which group consistently reports higher levels of satisfaction with their lives?
    a. married women
    b. married men
    c. single women
    d. single men

17. An important factor in increasing the chances for marital success?
    a. a desire to get married
    b. a desire to be married
    c. a fear of divorce
    d. marrying in your late twenties

18. Surveys find a tendency for more _____ and marital happiness to go together.
    a. frequent sexual intercourse
    b. money
    c. couples who cohabited prior to marriage
    d. total honesty in the relationship

19. Many people believe that trial marriages are a good way to discover

YOUR SPECIAL RELATIONSHIPS: LOVE AND MARRIAGE 101

compatiability prior to the commitment of marriage. When couples have cohabited prior to marriage their reported levels of satisfaction with the marriage is:
a. significantly higher than other couples
b. somewhat higher than other couples
c. the same as other couples
(d.) significantly lower than other couples

20. One of the life style adjustment problems of modern day marriages mentioned in your text?
a. who controls the finances
b. deciding how many children to have
(c.) who does the housework
d. arguing fairly

21. A 1984 survey showed that, regardless of age, length of marriage, or financial status, the overwhelming answer to the question "What do you argue most about" was:
a. relatives
(b.) money
c. children
d. personal freedom

22. In which type of marriage would you find a couple that is relatively content, has little or no conflict and who have separate interests?
a. devitalized
b. vital
(c.) passive-congenial
d. total

PEOPLE: HOW MUCH DO YOU KNOW?

Write what you can about the people listed below (as it relates to what you learned in this chapter).

Sternberg *Triangle Theory of love*

Walster and Walster *3 Conditions necessary for person to fall in love
1. culture
2. "right person"
3. physiological arousal interpreted as love*

102 YOUR WORLDS

Cuber and Harrof
Types of Marriages

Harlow

YOUR SPECIAL RELATIONSHIPS: LOVE AND MARRIAGE 103

PERSONAL GROWTH EXERCISE - YOUR LOVE TRIANGLES

PURPOSE To analyze the various components in the most important relationships in your life.

Step One Using Sternberg's Triangle of Love, draw the different love triangles in your life (parents, children, friend, significant other). Do not forget that a dotted line represents the dimentions which are missing from the relationship, and that you may have more than one per triangle. The longest line represents the most important component.

Step Two Do you find that you have dotted lines in some relationships where a continuous line would be more appropriate?   Yes _____   No _____

If you answered yes to the above question, does this tell you something about that relationship? What does it tell you?

Step Three If you do not like the shape of one of your triangles (or rather what it represents), can you think of ways in which you could change things? Is the relationship worth changing?

PERSONAL GROWTH EXERCISE - ARE YOU READY FOR LOVE?

PURPOSE To evaluate your present capacity to love another person, and your ability to maintain that love.

		Yes	No
1.	Are you a nice person?		
2.	Do you like yourself?		
3.	Do you enjoy: school		
4.	work		
5.	sports/exercise		
6.	hobbies		
7.	Do you often think about your strengths?		
8.	Do you often think about your weaknesses?		
9.	Are you a very shy person?		
10.	Are you an assertive person?		
11.	Did your parents praise you often?		
12.	Do people say negative things about you often?		
13.	Do you prefer to suppress your anger?		
14.	Are you suspicious of compliments?		
15.	Can you enjoy being alone?		
16.	Do you want a successful career?		
17.	Can you cook?		
18.	Can you do your own laundry?		
19.	Do you have at least one very good friend?		
20.	Are you frequently bored?		
21.	Have you ever lived away from home?		
22.	Do you "look at life through rose colored glasses?"		
23.	Do you often use defense mechanisms?		
24.	Do you sometimes use defense mechanisms?		
25.	Do you trust people easily?		
26.	Do you ever argue with friends?		
27.	Do you think that love is blind?		
28.	Do you try to change people?		
29.	If you don't get your own way, do you get upset?		
30.	Do arguments always upset you?		
31.	Do you always give in to others?		
32.	Do you never give in to others?		
33.	Do you often sulk?		
34.	Are you constantly in the minority?		
35.	Are other people often to blame for your problems?		
36.	Would you make major sacrifices for love?		
37.	Do you expect perfection from yourself?		
38.	Do you expect perfection from others?		
39.	Did your parents expect perfection from you?		
40.	Will losing weight solve many of your problems?		
41.	Will love make you happy?		
42.	If someone loves you should they change for you?		
43.	Do you avoid frustrating situations?		

YOUR SPECIAL RELATIONSHIPS: LOVE AND MARRIAGE

Scoring: Yes 1,2,3,4,5,6,7,11,15,16,17,18,19,21,24,25,26,36
          No 8,9,10,12,13,14,20,22,23,27,28,29,30,31,32,33,34,35,
              37,38,39,40,41,42,43

Give yourself 1 point for each "correct" answer

38-43 — You have the personal characteristics and maturity necessary to love and to maintain a successful love relationship - high self-esteem, ability to meet your own basic needs, contact with reality, the ability to deal with frustration, reasonable expectations.

27-37 — You have many of the personal characteristics and the maturity necessary to love another person and to maintain the relationship, but perhaps you need to work on one of the above characteristics.

15-26 — You are able to love another person, however, maintaining that relationship could be a problem for you. Review the above characteristics and work at increasing your chances for a good relationship.

less than 14 — Everyone is capable of giving and receiving love and of maintaining a good relationship. Some people have had more practice than others and some people are afraid of commitment and unconsciously place barriers between themselves and others. This could be you. Review Exhibit 8-1 in your text.

106 YOUR WORLDS

PERSONAL GROWTH EXERCISE - WHY DO YOU FALL IN LOVE?

PURPOSE   To ascertain what qualities you look for in the person you fall in love with, and what that suggests about your relationships.

It is important that you do NOT read through all of these questions prior to answering them - begin at the beginning and work through them.

Step One   Answer the following questions:

1. Are you in a serious relationship?   Yes _____   No _____

2. If yes, list the things you like most about your partner (if no you may use a past relationship for this exercise):

3. How many of the attributes you listed were physical? _____

4. How many of the attributes were social? _____

5. How many of the attributes were financial? _____

6. How many personal characteristics did you list? _____

7. List the things you dislike about your partner:

8. Have you tried to change your partner?   Yes _____   No _____

9. Do you believe that if he/she loves you they should change? Yes__ No__

10. Can you live with these things if he/she does not change?   Yes__ No__

   Studies have shown that as relationships mature, physical attributes become less important. With this in mind,

Step Two   Consider the following scenario:

Two very attractive couples are planning a wedding. Both couples have known each other for six months, have never had any serious problems during that time, but have weathered a few minor upsets. Both couples decide to go to pre-marriage counseling and the counselor asked each person to describe their partner. This is what the counselor heard:

   Jim: Suzie is so enthusiastic about everything that it's
         infectious. I just like being with her. She can make
         me feel good even when I've had a bad day.

Suzie: Jim is so supportive. When I was sick he brought me chicken soup. He is good with other people too, and he loves children. We both want children.

Jack: I have never felt the same way about any other girl before Jan, and I've dated lots of girls. I feel so good when I'm with her. She's really attractive and everyone says that we're the perfect couple.

Jan: Jack is so cute. He is taller than me and I like that because I am 5'9" and like to wear high heels. He has marvelous taste in clothes and always looks good. I hate slobs. I just love Jack so much.

Step Three Which couple do you think has the best opportunity of making their marriage work?

Why do you feel that way?

HINT Studies show that although physical attraction is a factor in the initial stages of a relationship, as that relationship matures and/or becomes more serious this aspect of the relationship becomes much less important and personal qualities are of more concern. Relationships which do not make this transition tend to remain superficial.

CHAPTER 9

The Worlds of Education and Work

LEARNING OBJECTIVES

1. To gain insight into why people go to college, and how they can make the most of the college experience.
2. How to choose an occupation which will interest you, which you will be good at, and which may be available where you want/need to work.
3. Understand the process of getting a job, to include finding prospects, doing well during the interview, and surviving those first days on a new job.

CHAPTER OUTLINE

I. THE WORLD OF EDUCATION
    A. Why Go To College?
        1. To postpone life decisions
        2. It is expected
        3. To become educated
        4. To get a better job
    B. Is College Worth It?
        1. A college degree was found to be a major determinant of income and occupational status (1979)
        2. School prestige is relatively unimportant for undergraduates
        3. School prestige is more important for graduate students
        4. 73% of highschool students, and 74% of their parents believe that college should teach something which will help them earn a living
        5. Vocationalism: colleges are moving away from a goal of educating people to one of training people
        6. College can provide: knowledge and new skills, lifelong friends, and a better chance at economic success

C. Adjusting To College
   1. This may be the first time away from home
   2. Students must become responsible for attending classes, study time, their own social life, etc.
D. Doing Well At College
   1. Make time for studying
      a. Schedule study time
      b. Don't leave studying until the day before an exam
      c. Distributed study time works better than massed study
   2. Study when you study:
      a. Accomplish something
      b. Concentrate on studying and don't become distracted (by t.v., eating, phone, children, friends)
      c. Cooperation from those you live with is important
      d. Study alone
   3. Improving your test scores
      a. Read all the directions
      b. Review the entire test before starting
      c. Make notes
      d. Answer all questions
      e. Use common sense
      f. Answer the question that is asked
      g. Outline answers if you run out of time (on essays)
      h. Spell correctly
   4. Reward yourself
      a. Lack of pressure will be a reward in itself but give yourself little rewards along the way
      b. A reward for a positive behavior (studying) does not rely on the outcome (the grade)
   5. Plan ahead: don't leave things until the last day
      a. Break down large assignments into more easily managed daily blocks
      b. If you want a free weekend, study a little more the week before (not after)
   6. Make a good impression
      a. What you do in class is important
      b. Impression management: go to class regularly, sit in the front of the class, be active, never ask "will this be on the test?" or "Are you covering anything important next week or it it o.k. if I miss class?", meet deadlines

II. THE WORLD OF WORK
    A. Choosing an Occupation
       1. What are you interested in?
          a. Interests can serve as a guide to future careers
          b. Interest inventory: questionnaires that allow you to compare your preferences and interests with those of people already employed in various occupations. This does not necessarily mean that you <u>will</u> be good at those jobs

2. What would you be good at?
   a. Abilities: basic physical, mental and psychological characteristics you must have to be able to learn to do something
   b. Skills: what you can already do
   c. If you have the ability you can learn the skill
   d. Campus counseling can help you get a better idea of your strengths and weaknesses
3. Finances
   a. Long training periods: can you afford to wait?
   b. Is the field saturated with qualified people already?
   c. What are the future employment opportunities?
   d. Will you face discrimination?
4. Where are the jobs?
   a. Future jobs: medical technology, computer graphics, robotics, fiber optics, telecommunications, energy, biotechnology
   b. Locations: west and southwest regions and Florida
5. What is the work like?
   a. Source book: the <u>Occupational Outlook Handbook</u> (Bureau of Labor Statistics
   b. Talk with someone employed in the field
   c. Take a summer job/part-time job in the field
   d. Become a volunteer and observe first hand
   e. Job satisfaction is an important part of life satisfaction
   f. It is often difficult to make major career changes once you are trained and on the way up the ladder

B. Getting a Job
   1. Finding prospects
      a. Help wanted signs: good for "just any job"
      b. Newspaper ads.: same as above but with more competition
      c. Employment agencies: might be expensive and time consuming
      d. Send resumes: a difficult way to get a job
      e. Visit company after company in person: a good way to get a job
      f. Use personal contacts: 40% of jobs are obtained this way
   2. Doing well at the interview
      a. You don't have to be a walking encyclopedia, but try to know something about the company
      b. Control your posture and body movements
      c. Avoid being overly formal or informal
      d. Vary your voice tone and facial expression
      e. Maintain eye contact
      f. Don't complain about former employers professors, or co-workers
      g. Be assertive about your talents
      h. Don't smoke

C. Career Development - A Process

1. Super and Hall's model of career development: descriptions of the stages people go through in their relationship with work:
   a. Growth Stage: fantasy
   b. Exploration Stage: trial and error
   c. Establishment Stage: growth
   d. Maintenance Stage: stability
   e. Decline Stage: shift of interests
2. Early career issues (establishment stage)
   a. People want to show what they can do
   b. Are interested in raises and promotion
   c. Often feel underemployed
   d. Importance: demonstrates effort, persistence, reliability, willingness, and the ability to work with others
   e. Try to stay one or two years
3. Resigning: leave politely and professionally
4. Middle career issues (maintenance stage)
   a. Changes in the job and in the organization can be frustrating and even frightening
   b. Some people begin to question old values, needs and priorities
5. Changing occupations - new challenges
   a. A change in life direction
   b. Have become more qualified
   c. Have been out of the workforce and must change jobs
   d. Changes are scary and exhilirating
   e. Be prepared before you change occupations, have goals, know what you want, study alternatives, be realistic

REVIEW QUESTIONS

MATCHING: Match the words and phrases below with the definitions

a. abilities
b. career development stages
c. distributed study
d. impression management
e. interest inventory
f. job satisfaction
g. massed study
h. skills
i. unfair discrimination
j. vocationalism

1. ___ Training people.
2. ___ Studying for five hours at one time.
3. ___ Breaking down study time into smaller units of time.
4. ___ Deliberate strategies which are used in order to present oneself in the best possible way.
5. ___ Questionnaire which allows you to compare your preferences and interests with those of people already employed in various occupations.
6. ___ The basic physical, mental and psychological characteristics you must have to be able to do something.

THE WORLDS OF EDUCATION AND WORK   113

7. ___ Things that you can already do.
8. ___ Preventing people from doing their job, or from obtaining a job or promotion on the basis of some non job-related characteristic.
9. ___ Super and Hall.
10. ___ Closely related to life-satisfaction.

PEOPLE YOU SHOULD KNOW

Freud
The Carnegie Foundation
Super and Hall

FILL-IN QUESTIONS

1. In order to be successful in college a student must make time for _____.

2. Studying for 2 hours a day rather than for 10 hours the day before an exam is an example of _____.

3. Many professors will give partial credit for a(n) _____ if you run out of time.

4. If you have a special project, one of the important things to remember to avoid last minute problems is _____.

5. Questionnaires which allow you to compare your preferences and interests with those of people already employed in various occupations is called _____.

6. _____ are what you can already do, and _____ is what it takes to learn to do something.

7. Many of the new jobs of the future will be located in the _____ and _____ regions, and in _____.

8. A good source book for information regarding what to expect (the necessary abilities, where you might find employment, facts about the work itself, working conditions and compensation) in hundreds of occupational fields is _____.

9. _____ means discriminating against people on the basis of some non job-related characteristic.

10. The best information about an occupation is obtained by _____.

11. In order to get a job, no matter how well qualified you are, it is important to _____.

TRUE-FALSE QUESTIONS

T F   1. A large scale study in 1979 found that a college degree was a major determinant of income and occupational status.

T F   2. The prestige of the college you attend for undergraduate work will be a major indication of the success you will achieve in life.

T F   3. The prestige of the college you attend for post graduate study will be an important variable for many persons.

T F   4. Many college students today graduate without knowing and without caring who and what were people such as Shakespeare, Einstein, and Leonardo de Vinci.

T F   5. Over 73 percent of high school students and their parents interviewed in a survey by the Carnegie Foundation agreed that learning something in college which would help them make a living is more important than "becoming educated."

T F   6. Massed study time is more effective than distributed study time.

T F   7. If you have an assignment to do for class(eg. a term paper) it is best to wait until you have a large block of time to devote to the project so that you can become absorbed in the work without distractions.

T F   8. How you behave in class is not important if you get your assignments in on time and turn up to take the tests.

T F   9. It is always a good idea to ask the professor if something is going to be on the next test so that you can be prepared.

T F   10. An interest profile that is drawn from a questionnaire called an interest inventory can show you how the things you like to do compare with the things you have to do in various occupations.

T F   11. Skills are the basic physical, mental and psychological characteristics you must have to be able to learn to do something.

T F   12. Being a good manager requires problem solving, decision-making, organizing, planning, and communication skills as well as technical skills in a particular field.

T F   13. Many of the new jobs of the future will be located in the west and southwest regions of the country, and in Florida.

T F   14. The Census Bureau estimates that a woman with five years or more of college will now earn as much meney as a man with the same qualifications.

THE WORLDS OF EDUCATION AND WORK

T F 15. Job satisfaction is an important part of life satisfaction.

T F 16. The best way to get a job is to send out lots of resumes to companies you are interested in working for.

T F 17. In an interview the best general strategy is to think of the situation as an exercise in impression management.

T F 18. If the person who is interviewing you for a job is smoking it is alright for you to do so.

T F 19. Most college graduates are disappointed with their first job following graduation.

MULTIPLE-CHOICE QUESTIONS

1. _____ is the traditional American route to job success.
   a. hard work
   b. education
   c. crime
   d. ability

2. In a large scale comprehensive study of economic success described in your text, what was found to be a major determinant of income and occupational status. (1979)
   a. high school diploma
   b. some college
   c. a college degree
   d. intelligence

3. The prestige of the college you attend is most important for which group of people?
   a. the post-graduate student
   b. the undergraduate student
   c. lawyers only
   d. all students

4. Leonardo da Vinci:
   a. developed the theory of evolution
   b. painted the ceiling of the Sistine Chapel
   c. was a 20th century painter
   d. none of the above

5. Studies have shown that a solid hour of study a day for 5 days will do more good than 5 hours of study at one time. What is this known as?
   a. study time spread
   b. associated study times
   c. distributed study time
   d. massed study time

116 YOUR WORLDS

6. If you are taking an exam and have only five minutes left to answer an essay question, what does your text suggest you do?
   a. write "no time to answer"
   b. ask for more time
   c. write as much as you can in the time you have
   d. outline your answer

7. An important factor in studying for an exam is to:
   a. not become distracted
   b. plan ahead
   c. reward yourself
   d. all of the above

8. Attending class regularly, sitting in the front of the room, answering questions in class, and meeting deadlines are all important aspects of:
   a. impression management
   b. college life
   c. the halo effect
   d. your self-concept

9. Questionnaires that allow you to compare your preferences and interests with those of people already employed in various occupations provides you with what?
   a. an interest inventory
   b. an interest profile
   c. a preference profile
   d. an occupation profile

10. As a general rule, the more your _____ suited to your chosen career, the more successful and satisfied you are likely to be.
    a. education is
    b. personality is
    c. abilities are
    d. vocationalism is

11. Which of the following is important for a successful manager?
    a. I take my time about making decisions
    b. I ignore "gut feelings"
    c. If I want something done right I must do it myself
    d. I have learned not to be a perfectionist about small, unimportant details

12. Which non job-related characteristic has been used to discriminate illegally against many people?
    a. race
    b. sex
    c. age
    d. all of the above

13. A woman with five or more years of college will make ___percent of

what a man will earn with the same or less education.
   a. 63
   b. 68
   c. 72
   d. 78

14. According to your text, the best way to obtain a job – other than directly through relatives and friends – is to:
    a. send out lots and lots of resumes
    b. visit company after company in person
    c. read the newspaper want ads.
    d. go to an employment agency

15. It is alright to smoke in a job interview if:
    a. the interviewer is smoking
    b. the interviewer offers you a cigarette
    c. you are very nervous and the interviewer is smoking
    d. never

16. Most people begin their work lives in earnest in young adulthood, concentrating on getting established. In Super and Hall's model of career development what is this stage characterized by?
    a. fantasy
    b. stability
    c. growth
    d. trial-and-error

PEOPLE: HOW MUCH DO YOU KNOW?

Write what you can about the people listed below (as it relates to what you learned in this chapter).

Freud

The Carnegie Foundation

118 YOUR WORLDS

Super and Hall

PERSONAL GROWTH EXERCISE - CHOOSING YOUR OCCUPATION

PURPOSE To help you to find out as much as you can about your choice of occupations.

1. Do you know what you want to do when you have completed college? What?

2. Have you ever worked in that field in any way (volunteer, part-time)?

3. Do you know someone who is successfully employed in that field?

4. Do you know someone who is not successful or is unhappy working in that field?

5. If possible, interview two people in the above catagories, and try to discover the reasons for the differences (eg. company they work for, qualifications, expectations, personality).

6. What are your expectations?
   salary $_____
   good hours _____
   personal satisfaction _____
   help others _____
   travel _____
   glamour _____
   power _____

7. Students often have very high expectations for their chosen career, especially in the area of financial rewards. Most college departments try to keep track of their graduates by sending out questionnaires from time to time asking for details about current employment and salary. Ask if your school does this, and if so, ask to see the results. You could be in for a shock. (In a recent survey of university graduates from a medium sized mid-western university only 7% of the students (social science) were making over $30,000 p.a., 23% were making between $20,000 and $29,999 p.a., 49% were making between $10,000 and $19,999 p.a., and 20% were making less than $10,000. This was a 1987 survey.)

8. Remember, "improving your chances of getting a better job" is an excellent reason for attending college, but don't just set your mind on the goal of "getting a degree and getting out." Try to relax, learn from, and enjoy the next three or four years, so that college life itself becomes a meaningful experience for you.

PERSONAL GROWTH EXERCISE - CAREER DEVELOPMENT

PURPOSE To help you to set up short term and long term goals which may result in positive career development.

1. Where do you want to be 5 years from now?

2. List two long term goals which will help you to get there:

3. List five short term goals which will help you to get there:

4. List five persoanlity characteristics which will help you to meet these goals:

5. Do you have any negative characteristics or circumstances which might prevent you from achieving your goals?

6. If so, how can you control for these variables?

7. Remember, it is never too soon to start to take charge of your own destiny. Fill out your resume as a senior, but live your resume right now! If you can't work part-time or full-time in a relevant career area, volunteer.

PERSONAL GROWTH EXERCISE - THE INTERVIEW

PURPOSE   To prepare you for one of the most stressful aspects of finding a new job - answering questions during the interview.

Expect to be asked one or more of the following questions, and prepare your answers in advance.

1. Why do you want to work for this company?

2. Why should we hire you?

3. What are your greatest strengths?
    a.
    b.
    c.
    d.
    e.

4. What are your greatest weaknesses?
    a.
    b.
    c.
    d.
    e.

    (Try to choose weaknesses which are, in fact, strengths. For example: "Sometimes I expect too much of others. I expect a great deal from myself and I just tend to expect other people to be the same.")

5. Tell me something about yourself.

6. Would you be willing to relocate?

7. What are your long term career goals?

8. What courses did you like best in college? Least? Why?

9. What kind of extra-curricular activities were you involved with?

10. Do you have any questions?

Practice interviewing with friends. Keep in mind that when you apply for a professional position you often have to undergo an interview by a panel not just by one person.

CHAPTER 10

Communication and Communicating

LEARNING OBJECTIVES

1. To understand the importance of effective communication and how it is obtained.

2. To be able to read nonverbal communications from others and to become aware of your own nonverbal communications.

3. To understand the special communication problems such as defensiveness, giving and receiving feedback, and assertiveness.

4. To learn how to listen to messages so that you really hear what the other person means, and are thus able to respond to the actual message that is being sent.

CHAPTER OUTLINE

I. UNDERSTANDING COMMUNICATION
   A. What is communication?
      1. Communication is a process whereby the behavior of one individual or group (the source) transmits some message to a second individual or group (the receiver)
      2. Interpersonal communication: takes place between two different individual parties
      3. Process: indicates movement initiated by the source
      4. Feedback: a reply to the first message
      5. One-way communication: when no feedback is transmitted
      6. Encoding: the behavior, verbal or nonverbal, which conveys a message from the source
      7. Channel: the observable form of encoding (Examples: a wink, a spoken sentence, a letter, a picture)

124 BASIC SKILLS FOR MORE EFFECTIVE BEHAVIOR

- 8. Decoding: the interpretation of the message by its receiver
- 9. For various reasons, the message sent (encoded) is not always the message received (decoded)

B. Effective Communication
1. Definition: communication that is received and acted upon (decoded) as intended (encoded)
2. Effective communication skills may be learned. None of these skills requires any special talents or individual attributes to master

C. Catagories (or Purposes) of Communication
1. Convey or elicit information: succeeds if the other party listens and understands and/or tells you what you want to know
2. Command or instruct: succeeds if the other person follows your orders/learns
3. Influence or persuade: succeeds if the other person acts accordingly
4. Clarify relationships: succeeds if the receiver accepts the message and behaves accordingly (many messages which are not intended to make a statement about a relationship may be interpreted that way (see examples in your text))
5. If you understand and keep in mind the various purposes of communication it will be easier for you to become an effective communicator

D. Undesired Effects of Communication
1. Surplus meaning: communicating something you did not intend as well as something you did
2. Relationship threats: communicating in a way which has negative effects on your relationship with your receiver
3. Bad timing: saying the right thing at the wrong time can have a negative effect on the situation

II. BASIC COMMUNICATION SKILLS
A. Limiting Noise
1. Definition of noise: anything that interferes with effective communication:
   a. Noise from the sender: when encoding the message or when sending the message
   b. Noise from the receiver
   c. Noise from the physical environment
   d. Noise from the social environment
   e. See Exhibit 10-1 in your text for examples

B. Choosing a Receiver
1. Try to communicate directly with the <u>appropriate</u> receiver
2. When this is not possible and leads to frustration:
   a. Find an appropriate outlet for your frustration (for example: a physical activity)
   b. Avoid displaced aggression (venting frustration on the wrong receiver)

C. Choosing the Channel

1. Face-to-face: best for influencing or persuading
2. Letter writing: time consuming
3. Leaving a note: convenient, but could be interpreted as an avoidance measure
4. Telephone: fast, convenient, provides instant gratification, feedback, and exchange of information
5. Electronic mail: information, letters, memos, etc. which show up on your personal computer not in your mailbox. Privacy is a problem
6. Telecommunications: combines the convenience of the telephone and the personal touch of the face-to-face contact

D. Encoding
  1. Definition of encoding: the actual words, symbols, gestures or other physical means by which you transmit your message
  2. Be clear
  3. Be precise
  4. Be complete
  5. Avoid slang or jargon unless you are sure your receiver will understand
  6. Be brief: only as long as necessary to get your point across

E. Avoid Loaded Words
  1. Definitions of loaded words: those words which carry a strong emotional meaning of their own over and above their context
  2. Loaded words are:
     a. Evaluative
     b. Judgemental
     c. Result in a defensive reaction
     d. Examples: always, never, fair, dumb, overreact, your problem is...

F. Be direct - But Not Blunt

G. Indirect Communication
  1. Definition: instead of saying what we really mean, we say something else and expect the receiver to break the code for our hidden message
  2. The "little white lie" is generally considered to be acceptable in certain situations, however, this is an ineffective means of communicating
  3. Indirect communication is often used to avoid huring someone's feelings or to be polite or tactful, but it is often annoying. (example: hinting)
  4. In certain situations, direct communication may not be appropriate (example: during a job interview)
  5. Potential risks of use: your receiver may not guess correctly what you are trying to say, you may be regarded as manipulative or "gamey" by others, you may appear uncertain about your message or lacking in self-confidence

H. Correct Timing
  1. Your receiver must be receptive (not busy, tired, ill, etc.)
  2. Salience: timing your messages so that they are received

126 BASIC SKILLS FOR MORE EFFECTIVE BEHAVIOR

           close to the time when the information is most relevant or must be acted upon
       3. Plan ahead: do not wait until the last minute to communicate especially if you need feedback
  I. Making Your Messages Stand Out
       1. Unless your message is noticed, heard, seen, or read it will not be effective
       2. Advertisers are skillful in making messages stand out. (examples: loud music, fast speech, soft speech, animation, large letters, bright colors)
  J. Soliciting Feedback
       1. Don't assume that your message was received and/or understood
       2. If it is important, follow up on it in person

III. NONVERBAL COMMUNICATION
  A. Definition: messages sent via posture, gestures, facial expressions, touching, voice tone, and other "not speech" behaviors that can be observed by those with whom we are interacting
       1. As much as 90% of communication in some situations may take place nonverbally
       2. Some nonverbal messages stand alone and are easily understood
       3. Some nonverbal messages reinforce verbal messages
       4. Some nonverbal messages contradict verbal messages
  B. Reading Nonverbal
       1. Nonverbal communication is a very imprecise language and is subject to a variety of interpretations
       2. Emphasis and tone of voice can change the nature of the message received
  C. Speaking Nonverbal
       1. Be aware that your intended message could be misunderstood
       2. Mastering this language to your advantage is difficult
       3. Experts disagree on the meanings of nonverbal language
       4. Rules for nonverbal communication:
          a. Try to rid yourself of any nonverbal habits that show nervousness
          b. Learn to maintain eye contact when speaking to others
          c. Act on any consistent feedback you receive about your nonverbal communications
          d. Relax

IV. SPECIAL COMMUNICATION SITUATIONS
  A. Defensiveness: can distort the message received
       1. Sources:
          a. Something the source says or does (for example voice tone)
          b. Something in the relationship between the source and and the receiver (for example: past disagreements)

COMMUNICATION AND COMMUNICATING 127

        Can be the most difficult to combat, and is often a continuing problem in marital communications
      c. Something about the receiver (for example: receiver's bad mood)
- B. Reducing Defensiveness
  1. Be careful about the way you say things:
     a. Ask a negative question
     b. Own your own feelings, opinions, perceptions
     c. Send "I" messages rather than "you" messages
     d. Be tentative rather than dogmatic
     e. Don't imply that you are superior
     f. Don't generalize from one situation to a person's entire personality or behavior patterns
     g. Send to the appropriate receiver
     h. Use the appropriate channel
     i. Be clear and direct
     j. Time your message correctly
     k. Solicit feedback
- C. Feedback (Evaluations)
  1. Giving feedback
     a. Be direct
     b. Be descriptive, not evaluative
     c. Be specific
     d. Be constructive
     e. Be positive as well as negative
     f. Be quiet - don't give evaluations unless asked
  2. Receiving feedback - if you don't want any feedback, don't ask any questions. If you do want genuine feeback, don't ask pseudoquestions
  3. Definition of pseudoquestions: a form of indirect communication which we use when we really want to say something else or to get someone to agree with us. Types of psuedoquestions:
     a. Cooptive
     b. Got'cha
     c. Hypothetical
     d. Imperative
     e. Punitive
     f. Rhetorical
     g. Set-up
     h. See Exhibit 10-7 of your text for examples
- D. Assertiveness
  1. Assertive behavior: behavior that expresses your personal feelings or opinions or helps you accomplish your goals in spite of the disagreement or opposition of others. Not aggressiveness (hostile, injurious, destructive, disrespectful of the rights of others)
  2. The Ten Word Response: point out what is unsatisfactory to you about the situation and offer an alternative in ten words of less
  3. The Broken Record Technique: repeat your assertive phrase

128 BASIC SKILLS FOR MORE EFFECTIVE BEHAVIOR

      in exactly the same calm, matter-of-fact tone as many times as it takes to change the situation
    4. Fogging: clouding the issue so as to avoid a confrontation
    5. Assertiveness takes practice and gets easier every time (practice role-playing situations with a friend)
  E. Listening
    1. Receiving a message:
      a. Open your ears and your mind
      b. Look at the sender
      c. Try not to interrupt
      d. Avoid preoccupation:
        i. you think you know what the speaker will say
        ii. you are not very interested
        iii. you are rehearsing what you will say next
        iv. you are distracted by a task
    2. Hearing the message (with understanding)
      a. Avoid surface listening: when you hear only the spoken words and not the actual message
      b. Avoid selective listening: when you hear only what you want or expect to hear
      c. Concentrate
      d. Listen actively
    3. Responding to the message
      a. Pause before you reply
      b. Acknowledge the speaker's message
      c. Don't play "I can top that"
      d. Don't change the subject
      e. Check your understanding of the message (you may use Rogers' "Say Back" technique described in this chaper of your text):
        i. "Say Back" - you paraphrase what you thought your speaker meant and allow him or her to confirm or clarify your understanding of the message

REVIEW QUESTIONS

MATCHING: Match the words and phrases below with the definitions

a. active listening
b. agressiveness
c. channel
d. decode
e. displaced aggression

f. effective communication
g. fogging
h. loaded words
i. negative question
j. noise

1. _d_ The interpretation of the message by the receiver.
2. _c_ The observable form of communication - a wink, a spoken sentence, a letter, or a picture.
3. _f_ Communication that is received and acted upon as intended.
4. _j_ Anything that interferes with effective communication.
5. _e_ Venting frustration on the wrong receiver.

COMMUNICATION AND COMMUNICATING   129

- _h_ Words that carry strong meanings of their own over and and above their context.
- _i_ "I don't suppose you've seen my white shirt anywhere, have you?"
- _g_ Clouding the issue so as to avoid a confrontation.
- _a_ Opening your ears and your mind, listening for the real message in context, and checking the meaning if you have doubts.
- _b_ Venting frustration in an inappropriate manner.

PEOPLE YOU SHOULD KNOW

Aristotle   Pfeiffer and Jones   Mehrabian
Lakoff   Buffington
Kim   Rogers

FILL-IN QUESTIONS

1. The interpretation of the message by the receiver is called the _decoding_.

2. If the receiver does not transmit feedback, we say that _one-way comm_ has occurred.

3. _effective_ communication is communication that is received and acted upon as intended.

4. The two major catagories of undesired side effects of interpersonal communication are _surplus meaning_ and _relationships threat_.

5. In communication terminology, anything that interferes with effective communication is called _noise_.

6. Venting frustration on the wrong receiver is called _displaced aggression_.

7. A very popular communication channel today is _telephone_.

8. Words that carry strong emotional meanings of their own over and above their context are known as _loaded words_.

9. _men_ interrupt more than _women_ in conversation between mixed sex groups.

10. _salient_ means timing your messages so that they are received close to the time when the information will be most relevant.

11. _nonverbal comm_ refers to messages sent via postures, gestures, facial expressions, touching, voice tone, and other "not speech" behaviors.

12. The feedback loop in the basic communication process may be used to

130 BASIC SKILLS FOR MORE EFFECTIVE BEHAVIOR

check that your receiver has understood your message, but the word feedback may also refer to _evaluation_

13. Traps or set-ups which close off receiver options for reply are known as _pseudoquestion_

14. _fogging_ is a way of clouding the issue so as to avoid confrontation.

15. _hearing_ means understanding what the speaker is trying to communicate.

16. Being a good listener, listening for the real messages, and checking the meaning if you have doubts are all behaviors involved in _active listening_.

TRUE-FALSE QUESTIONS

(T) F 1. Communicating effectively requires a set of skills which can be learned.

(T) F 2. Both the source and the receiver of a message can be groups as well as individuals.

(T) F 3. Communication is best conceptualized as a process.

T (F) 4. The interpretation of a message by the receiver is known as encoding.

(T) F 5. In order to determine whether communication is effective or ineffective requires that we know the intent of the communicator.

T (F) 6. Communication to clarify relationships succeeds if the receiver listens and understands the message.

T (F) 7. In communication terminology, anything that interferes with effective communication is called surplus meaning.

(T) F 8. Noise can originate with the source or the receiver as well as in the channel.

(T) F 9. Venting frustration on the wrong receiver is known as displaced aggression.

(T) F 10. The very choice of one channel over another can send a message of its own.

(T) F 11. In a communication context, salience means timing messages so that they are received close to the time when the information they contain will be relevant or must be acted upon.

T (F) 12. Messages sent via posture, gestures, facial expressions, touching, voice tone, and other "not speech" behaviors that can be observed by those with whom we are interacting are known as indirect communication.

(T) F 13. Nonverbal communication can either reinforce or contradict verbal messages.

(T) F 14. The feedback loop in the basic communication process may be used to check that your receiver has heard your message and understood it as you intended.

T (F) 15. Pseudoquestions are a form of direct communication.

T (F) 16. Assertive behavior is behavior which is hostile, injurious, or destructive toward others.

T (F) 17. Surface listening means hearing only what you expect to hear or want to hear.

(T) F 18. Understanding others is an active not a passive process.

MULTIPLE-CHOICE QUESTIONS

1. The process whereby the behavior of one individual or group transmits some message to a second individual or group.
    a. transmission
    b. encoding
    c. relaying
    (d.) communication

2. Communication is a:
    a. channel
    (b.) process
    c. noise
    d. response

3. If the receiver does not _____ we say that one-way communication has occurred.
    a. understand
    b. listen actively
    (c.) transmit feedback
    d. decode the message

4. What is the interpretation of the communication by the receiver called?
    (a.) decoding
    b. encoding
    c. recoding
    d. channeling

132 BASIC SKILLS FOR MORE EFFECTIVE BEHAVIOR

5. Even if we do not wish to communicate, we all communicate via:
   a. pseudo behavior
   b. surface behavior
   c. nonverbal behavior
   d. fogging

6. What is communication which is received and decoded as encoded called?
   a. effective
   b. ineffective
   c. nonverbal
   d. secretive

7. Communication may be used to:
   a. elicit information
   b. influence
   c. command
   d. all of the above

8. A communicated message that has more to it when it is decoded than it had when it was encoded is said to have:
   a. displaced decoding
   b. surplus meaning
   c. loaded encoding
   d. surface meaning

9. Which of the following could unintentionally lead to relationship threats in your communication with a friend?
   a. timing
   b. defensive encoding
   c. aggressive encoding
   d. negative feedback

10. Which of the following would NOT be considered to be "noise" in the communication process?
    a. vague message
    b. poor phone connection
    c. scrambled t.v. reception
    d. all are noise

11. If your room-mate's mother sends you a gift for Christmas and you thank your room-mate at the beginning of the spring semester, this is an example of:
    a. choosing the wrong receiver
    b. waiting too late to say "Thank you"
    c. ineffective communication
    d. fogging

12. You are late and can't find your car keys. Your room-mate/spouse comes into the room and tells you to think of what you did as soon as you arrived home last night and you will probably find the keys

there. You snap at him/her. What is this an example of?
   a. ineffective communication
   b. assertive behavior
   c. anger
   d. displaced aggression

13. What is the method of channeling which has increased dramatically over the past 20 years?
    a. nonverbal
    b. telephoning
    c. selective listening
    d. active listening

14. According to your text, what is a major problem with loaded words?
    a. they are evaluative
    b. they are ineffective
    c. they are defensive
    d. they are aggressive

15. Instead of saying what we really mean, we often say something else and expect the receiver to break the code in our message. What is this kind of communication known as?
    a. poor
    b. indirect
    c. nonverbal
    d. one-way

16. In mixed-sex groups, who dominated the conversation?
    a. males in general
    b. females in general
    c. the most attractive males
    d. the most attractive females

17. Which of the following is described in your text as a method of communication used often by advertisers?
    a. making messages stand out
    b. soliciting feedback
    c. salience
    d. all of the above

18. According to Mehrabian, what percent of communication in some situations may take place via nonverbal messages?
    a. 90
    b. 80
    c. 72
    d. 68

19. If you say "I feel hurt when I am not consulted about our plans for the evening" instead of "You never ask me what I'd like to do," you are using a communication technique which tends to do what?
    a. displace aggression

134 BASIC SKILLS FOR MORE EFFECTIVE BEHAVIOR

      b. increase defensiveness
      (c.) reduce defensiveness
      d. increase aggression

20. Co-optive, got'cha, hypothetical, imperative, punitive, rhetorical, set-up, are all types of what?
      a. loaded words
      (b.) pseudoquestions
      c. preoccupation
      d. fogging

21. If you respect the rights of others but do not allow yourself to be intimidated or inhibited by challenges, disapproval from others, or fears of making a scene, what kind of person are you likely to be?
      a. aggressive
      b. positive
      c. courageous
      (d.) assertive

22. "You are out of order. I was next." What is this an example of?
      a. one-way communication
      (b.) the ten word response
      c. the broken record technique
      d. aggressive behavior

23. "You know, you could be right." What is this an example of?
      a. the ten word response
      b. the broken record technique
      (c.) fogging
      d. clouding

24. According to your text, what is one of the major blocks to reception of a communication?
      (a.) preoccupation
      b. fogging
      c. active listening
      d. response blocking

PEOPLE: HOW MUCH DO YOU KNOW?

Write what you can about the people listed below (as it related to what you learned in this chapter).

Umstot

Lakoff

Ayim

Pfeiffer and Jones

Buffington

Rogers

136 BASIC SKILLS FOR MORE EFFECTIVE BEHAVIOR

PERSONAL GROWTH EXERCISE - LOADED WORD ACTIVITY

PURPOSE To alert you to the dangers of using loaded words in your communications with someone who is important to you.

1. List some key words or phrases that signal danger or trouble in your relationship with a significant other (parent, friend, spouse):

   a. Things you say which make him/her react:

   b. Things he/she says which make you react:

2. Think of an incident when you and your significant other had an argument due to your misunderstanding of his or her intent. Was there anything in the exchange prior to the argument that might have alerted you to his or her feelings - loaded words, tone of voice, body language, etc.?

3. What can/will you do to avoid arguments with this person in the future?

4. If there are certain words or phrases which always make you "see red," have you discussed this with the important people in your life? If you have not done so, and decide to do so after reading this, don't forget to use "I" and "me" sentences rather than "you" sentences!

COMMUNICATION AND COMMUNICATING   137

PERSONAL GROWTH EXERCISE - READING NONVERBAL

PURPOSE To become more aware of how nonverbal behavior can influence the way other people react to you, and how their nonverbal behavior influences how you react to them.

Step One Think of someone you know. List the nonverbal behaviors which would indicate to you that person's mood

a. Person _____
   Mood: Happy
   Behavior _____

b. Person _____
   Mood: Angry
   Behavior _____

c. Person _____
   Mood: Depressed
   Behavior _____

Step Two Think of two people that you know. Do they have a positive relationship or a negative relationship? List the nonverbal behaviors that indicate this relationship to outsiders. Repeat the exercise using the opposite type of relationship.

a. Friends _____
   Relationship _____
   Behaviors _____
   _____

b. Friends _____
   Relationship _____
   Behaviors _____
   _____

138 BASIC SKILLS FOR MORE EFFECTIVE BEHAVIOR

Step Three If you are involved in a serious relationship, repeat the last exercise. Do the other person's everyday behaviors indicate a positive relationship exists between the two of you?

    Relationship _____

    Behaviors _____

    _____

    _____

(Sometimes we become involved in relationships which are not in our best interests, but we cannot or will not see the negative aspects of the relationship. We do an effective job of fooling ourselves, or else are fooled by the other person. By learning to pay attention to nonverbal behaviors we can often tell the difference between a positive and a negative relationship.)

Step Four Repeat the last exercise, but this time record your own everyday behaviors.

    Relationship _____

    Behaviors _____

    _____

    _____

(Sometimes we fool ourselves that we are "in love with" a particular person, but no matter how many times we tell ourselves that this is true our own nonverbal behaviors can give us away.)

PERSONAL GROWTH EXERCISE - LACK OF COMMUNICATION

PURPOSE   To understand the extent of damage caused by a lack of communication.

Step One   Try to watch one of the daytime "soaps" for one week.

Step Two   List the number of times someone in the show misunderstands another person's communication, refuses to communicate important information to a loved one, lies to someone, tells the wrong person something important, uses loaded words, or is not direct in what they are saying.

Step Three   When the above mistakes in communication are made by someone else, especially by someone on t.v. or in the movies, we can all see how foolish the situation is. Why do you think we don't see as clearly when we are one of the actors in our own drama?

140 BASIC SKILLS FOR MORE EFFECTIVE BEHAVIOR

PERSONAL GROWTH EXERCISE - METHODS OF COMMUNICATION

PURPOSE   To become aware of why you choose various methods of communication.

We all have several options available to us when we wish to communicate with another person. Have you ever thought about how your choice of HOW you send your message can be a nonverbal communication in itself?

Step One   What is your communication method of choice when you have to talk with:

a. friends

b. parents

c. distant relatives

d. significant other

e. professor

f. boss

Step Two   In the following situations, what method of communication would you use?

a. You are going to be late for a date, dinner, a meeting

b. You want to make a doctor's appointment

c. You have to cancel a date with someone very special to you

d. You have to tell someone that their spouse has been injured in an accident

e. You are going to tell your husband that you are going to have a baby or
f. If your wife is going to tell you that she is going to have a baby how would you like to be told?

g. You must tell your boss that you need a day off work

h. You quit work

i. You want to wish someone a Merry Christmas

CHAPTER 11
Decisions and Decision Making

LEARNING OBJECTIVES

1. Define decision, and identify the elements of decision making.

2. Outline ways to make better decisions.

3. Learn to live with your decisions once they have been made.

CHAPTER OUTLINE

I. ELEMENTS OF DECISION MAKING
   A. The Decision: is the decision major, novel, complex, or problematic?
   B. The decision maker: what are your needs, values, goals, and priorities?
   C. The environment of the decision: the physical conditions and social context wither which the decision is made.

II. THE DECISION
   A. Definition of a decision: that which is required of you when you must choose between two or more alternatives.
   B. Factors influencing a decision include:
      1. Number of alternative courses of action
      2. Whether or not there is a problem involved
   C. Definition of a problem: an obstacle to a goal. To solve a problem you must answer three questions:
      1. What is the obstacle?
      2. How did it get there (or what is causing it)?
      3. What course of action (alternatives) might remove it or cut it down to size?

III. THE DECISION MAKER
   A. Needs and Decision Making
      1. Motivation: the sum of the forces that energize, direct, and maintain your behavior
      2. Motivation can be caused by psychological as well as physical needs
   B. Goals and Decision Making
      1. Goal: an end toward which people will expend effort. Useful goals need to be clear, measurable, and attainable
      2. Goal conflict: occurs when behaviors required to accomplish several goals are in conflict. Lewin has identified:
         a. Approach-approach conflict: when you are motivated to strive toward each of two goals that are both attractive, but don't seem to be simultaneously attainable
         b. Approach-avoidance conflict: the same goal has both attractive and unattractive features
            i. goal gradients (the relative strength of a goal as we are closer to it or farther from it) can produce a form of indecision known as vacillation
         c. Avoidance-avoidance conflict: occurs when you must decide between two equally unattractive prospects. It frequently results in putting off actually making a decision
         d. Double approach-avoidance conflict: the most complex kind of goal conflict in which you must choose between two goals, each of which has positive and negative features
   C. Cognitive Processes (how you think) and Decision Making
      1. Decision-making style: the information processing approach that characterizes the way a person goes about making decisions
      2. Decision making styles (which vary according to the amount of information used and the number of alternative choices developed) include the following:
         a. Decisive decision makers: they use a relatively small amount of information to come up with a small number of alternatives
         b. Integrative decision makers: they collect a great deal of information and generate a large number of alternatives before making a decision
         c. Flexible decision makers: they generate many alternatives out of limited information
         d. Hierarchic decision makers: they use a lot of information to generate only a few alternatives

IV. THE ENVIRONMENT OF DECISIONS
   A. Decision Making and the Physical Environment
      1. Better decisions are made when your physical surroundings are comfortable
      2. A little forethought will help you avoid hostile physical

conditions wither which a decision must be made
- B. Decision Making and the Social Environment
  1. Because your decisions do not always involve you alone, society becomes involved in your decision making by providing the following:
     a. Constraints
     b. Norms
     c. Demands

V. MAKING BETTER DECISIONS
- A. Maximizing versus Satisficing
  1. Definition of maximizing: a rational decision making strategy that emphasizes making the best possible decision
  2. Definition of satisficing: making a "good enough" decision
- B. Defining the Task (the first step in decision making) and setting decision criteria (which are used to evaluate the decision you make)
- C. Collecting Information
  1. Maximizing requires that you have all the relevant information and this is seldom possible
  2. There is always a gap (called uncertainty) between the information you have and perfect information
  3. Decisions made under uncertainty entail risk
  4. Even a simple decision can generate information overload (more information than we can deal with at one time)
- D. Organizing Information
  1. Formal techniques for organizing information are called decision aids
  2. A decision tree is a decision aid which allows you to organize information relevant to a decision

VI. LIVING WITH YOUR DECISIONS
- A. Postdecisional Regret
  1. Definition of postdecisional regret: doubts about your choice or a wish that you had made a different decision
  2. Hot cognitions: Abelson's term which refers to thoughts about vital issues which have long-term or important personal consequences and can't be redone, or undone, easily
  3. Janis and Mann believe that learning to anticipate sources of postdecisional regret is critical to dealing successfully with it
- B. The Decisional Balance Sheet
  1. A written summary of the various kinds of gains and losses that you anticipate will follow your decision alternatives
  2. The balance sheet technique helps to prepare you for possible negative consequences of your decision
  3. Janis and Mann call the effect of advance warning the innoculation hypothesis

144 BASIC SKILLS FOR MORE EFFECTIVE BEHAVIOR

    C. Changing Your Mind
       1. Like other decisions, changing your mind will have gains and losses for you and possibly for others
       2. Every situation will be a little different, but a good rule to follow is to give yourself permission in advance to change your mind

REVIEW QUESTIONS

MATCHING: Match the words and phrases below with the definitions

a. constraints on decision making
b. demands on decision making
c. decision
d. decision making style
e. decision tree
f. double approach-avoidance conflict
g. goal
h. goal gradient
i. hot cognitions
j. satisficing

1. __c__ When you must choose between one or more alternatives.
2. __g__ An end toward which people will exert effort.
3. __h__ The relative strength of a goal as we are closer to it or farther from it.
4. __f__ The most complex kind of goal conflict where you must choose between two goals, each of which has positive and negative features.
5. __d__ The information processing approach that characterizes the way we go about making decisions.
6. __a__ Because your decisions do not always involve you alone, society sometimes has an impact on the decision you make.
7. __b__ Other people have expectations for what you decide and your relationships can be affected if you ignore these expectations.
8. __j__ Making "good enough" decisions.
9. __e__ A decision aid.
10. __i__ Decisions which have long-term or important personal consequences and which have a greater chance of creating postdecisional regret.

PEOPLE YOU SHOULD KNOW

Lewin
Driver and Rowe
Abelson
Janis and Mann

Festinger
Simon

FILL-IN QUESTIONS

1. A _decision_ is required of you when you must choose between one or more alternatives.

DECISIONS AND DECISION MAKING   145

2. A _problem_ is an obstacle to a goal.

3. Much of your behavior is not motivated by physical needs, but by _psychological_ needs.

4. A large body of research leaves no doubt that both school and work performance improve when people have _clear_, _measurable_ and _attainable_ goals.

5. Because your decisions do not always involve you alone, society places certain _constraints_ on your decision making.

6. _Maximizing_ is a rational decision making strategy that emphasizes making the best possible decision. By contrast, _satisficing_ is making a "good enough" decision.

7. The truth is that human beings have _cognitive limits_ when it comes to information processing. We can deal with only so much information at a time.

8. Post decisional _regret_ refers to doubts about your choice or a wish that you had made a different decision.

9. A decisional _balance sheet_ is a written summary of the various kinds of gains and losses that you anticipate will follow your major decision alternatives.

10. Changing your mind about a decision you have made is in itself a _decision_ and it can be a difficult one to make.

11. _Maximizing_ is a rational decision making strategy that emphasizes making the best possible decision.

12. While you are defining your decision task, it also helps to _set the criteria_ by which you will evaluate the decision you make.

13. There is a gap between the information you have and perfect information, and this gap is called _uncertainty_.

14. Even a simple decision can generate _information overload_, more information than we can deal with at one time.

15. Human beings have _cognitive limits_ when it comes to information processing. We can deal with only so much information at a time.

16. Formal techniques for organizing information are called _decision aids_ and an example of this would be a _decision tree_.

17. _Hot cognitions_ make you more vulnerable to being influenced by negative information, and to suffering postdecisional regret.

146 BASIC SKILLS FOR MORE EFFECTIVE BEHAVIOR

TRUE-FALSE QUESTIONS

(T) F 1. All problems require you to make decisions if they are to be solved, but not all decisions involve problems.

(T) F 2. The individual characteristics of the decision maker play an important role in decision making.

T (F) 3. The sum of all the forces that energize, direct, and maintain your behavior are known as needs. *motivation*

(T) F 4. Much of your behavior is not motivated by physical needs, but by psychological needs.

(T) F 5. Psychological needs affect your ability to evaluate information.

T (F) 6. An end toward which people will exert effort is known as a need.

(T) F 7. In order to be useful a goal must be attainable.

T (F) 8. Only unclear goals can come into conflict with each other.

T (F) 9. In an approach-avoidance conflict, two goals have both attractive and unattractive features.

(T) F 10. Psychologists have found that people are inconsistent in their reactions to approach-avoidance conflicts.

(T) F 11. The relative strength of a goal as we are closer to it or farther from it is called a goal gradient.

(T) F 12. The feeling one gets when holding ideas that are inconsistent with one another is known as dissonance.

(T) F 13. A person who feels that he or she is "between a rock and a hard place" is experiencing avoidance-avoidance conflict.

(T) F 14. The most complex kind of goal conflict is the double approach-avoidance conflict.

T (F) 15. Research indicates that more intelligent people make better decisions than people with lower intelligence.

(T) F 16. Other things being equal, you will make more satisfactory decisions when your physical surroundings are comfortable and reasonably quiet and you are not pressed for time.

(T) F 17. Maximizing is a rational decision making strategy that emphasizes making the best possible decision.

DECISIONS AND DECISION MAKING 147

(T) F 18. Decisions made under uncertainty entail risk.

T (F) 19. A person can never have too much information when making a decision.

(T) F 20. Most people lack the time and cognitive abilities to be perfectly rational decision makers.

MULTIPLE-CHOICE QUESTIONS

1. Which of the following is NOT one of the three elements involved in every decision?
   a. the decision itself
   b. previous decisions
   c. the decision maker
   d. the environment of the decision

2. The sum of the forces that energize, direct, and maintain your behavior is called:
   a. goal orientation
   b. a need
   c. motivation
   d. dissonance

3. Which of the following does NOT have to be present in order for a goal to be useful?
   a. clarity
   b. measurability
   c. attainability
   d. immediacy

4. When you are motivated to strive toward each of two goals that are both attractive, but don't seem to be simultaneously attainable, you experience what kind of conflict?
   a. approach-approach
   b. approach-avoidance
   c. avoidance-avoidance
   d. non of the above

5. The effect of the approach and avoidance goal gradient upon decision making is to create a form of indecision. What is this called?
   a. ambiguity
   b. dissonance
   c. vacillation
   d. satisficing

6. Who, among the following, originated the theory of cognitive dissonance?
   a. Selye
   b. Festinger

148 BASIC SKILLS FOR MORE EFFECTIVE BEHAVIOR

      c. Simon
      d. Lewin

7. Psychologists who study decision making say that each of us has a decision making style that varies according to:
      a. the amount of information used
      b. the number of alternative choices developed
      (c.) both of the above
      d. neither of the above

8. Who, among the following, developed the distinction between maximizing and satisficing in the decision making process?
      (a.) Simon
      b. Festinger
      c. Driver and Rowe
      d. Lewin

9. Having more information than we can deal with at one time is known as information:
      a. processing
      b. reduction
      c. uncertainty
      (d.) overload

10. What are formal techniques for organizing information called?
      a. decision maximizers
      (b.) decision aids
      c. decision synthesizers
      d. decision criteria

11. Who, among the following, believe(s) that learning to anticipate sources of postdecisional regret is critical in handling its outcome?
      a. Festinger
      b. Lewin
      (c.) Janis and Mann
      d. Driver and Rowe

PEOPLE: HOW MUCH DO YOU KNOW?

Write what you can about the people listed below (as it relates to what you learned in this chapter).

Lewin

Driver and Rowe

Abelson

Janis and Mann

Festinger

Simon

150 BASIC SKILLS FOR MORE EFFECTIVE BEHAVIOR

PERSONAL GROWTH EXERCISE - YOUR DECISION MAKING STYLE

PURPOSE To determine your decision making style.

Step One Recall a recent decision of some importance that you were required to make.

Step Two List all of the information you used in making the decision:

Step Three How many alternatives did you generate?

a. Approach:

b. Avoidance:

Step Four Based upon the amount of information gathered and number of alternatives generated you should now be able to determine your decision making style. If necessary, consult Figure 11-4 in your text for confirmation or review.

DECISIONS AND DECISION MAKING   151

PERSONAL GROWTH EXERCISE - WHERE DO YOU MAKE YOUR DECISIONS?

PURPOSE To determine the location in which you make most of your decisions, and to evaluate your selection of location.

Step One   Recall and list at least four decisions that you have been required to make recently:

a.

b.

c.

d.

Step Two   Describe the location in which you made each of the decisions. Was the location:

a. quiet or noisy

b. crowded or secluded

c. neat or cluttered

d. warm or cold

e. familiar or unfamiliar

f. other characteristics of the location

Step Three   Considering the information presented in this chapter of your text, do you feel that you are making your decisions in the best possible surroundings?
                       Yes _____   No _____

If no, list and describe at least two more desirable locations that are available to you for use in making future decisions:

a.

b.

The next time you have a decision to make, try to do so in one of these alternative locations and see if you find it easier to weigh all of the possible options open to you.

CHAPTER 12
Stress and Stress Management

LEARNING OBJECTIVES

1. Define stress, identify both environmental and psychological stressors in your life, and learn successful stress management techniques.

2. Outline ways in which you can make more efficient use of your time via time management skills.

CHAPTER OUTLINE

I. WHAT IS STRESS?
   A. Definitions:
      1. Stress: a significant departure from an individual adapted state.
      2. Stressor: an event or condition that has the potential to create departures from the adapted state.
         a. External
         b. Internal
   B. Stress as:
      1. A reaction to a stimulus event - "I am stressed out"
      2. A stimulus - "I am under great stress"
      3. A relationship between an individual and the environment.
   C. Environmental Stressors (external): noise, temperature, time.
   D. Life Events:
      1. Any change, whether positive or negative, can lead to stress.
      2. Events and changes which are more likely to cause psychological problems are:
         a. Negative events
         b. Events perceived as beyond control
         c. Example: death of a loved one

E. Psychological Stressors.
    1. Frustration: the blocking of goal oriented behavior.
        a. External: an employer promotes a friend instead of you, you can't find your car keys, traffic problems.
        b. Internal: you are shy and this prevents you from speaking up in class, you have set unrealistic goals for yourself and cannot meet them.
    2. Perceived Pressure:
        a. External: your parents expect you to do well in college, your friends want to party and you want to study.
        b. Internal: ambition, insecurity, guilt (you partied and did not study).

II. REACTIONS TO STRESSORS - PHYSICAL
    A. Hans Selye's General Adaptation Syndrome: physical changes that accompany stress. There are three stages:
        1. Alarm Stage: (fight or flight) the body is alerted to action to help meet a challenge - increased blood pressure and metabolism, the release of certain hormones, cessation of the digestive processes, tensed muscles, kidneys retain water, the immune system shuts down.
        2. Resistance Stage: the body tries to adapt to the new state of affairs (using coping techniques and/or defense mechanisms), it works at high efficiency but cannot do so for an extended period.
        3. Exhaustion Stage: if you have not reduced or eliminated the perceived threat, coping mechanisms used in the previous stage begin to fail due to resource depletion. Continued exposure to stress at this stage may result in damage to your previous level of functioning.
    B. Stress and Illness. Psychophysiological Problems: long-term or multiple stressors can result in: heart disease, tuberculosis, allergies, cancer, hives, ulcers, asthma, migraine headaches.

III. REACTIONS TO STRESSORS - PSYCHOLOGICAL
    A. Defense Mechanisms (Freud): psychological responses that cushion the blow when we experience stress. They are:
        1. Normal, and to a large degree unconscious.
        2. Helpful in handling a severe stressor in the short-run, but only until appropriate coping skills can be mobilized.
        3. Not healthy as a long-term method of dealing with stress.
        4. Types (see Exhibit 12-1 in the text):
            a. Denial
            b. Projection
            c. Fantasizing
            d. Intellectualization
            e. Regression
            f. Repression
            g. Displacement
            h. Ventilation

STRESS AND STRESS MANAGEMENT 155

IV. DISTRESS VERSUS EUSTRESS
   A. Distress: results when the energy created by stress is not used positively.
   B. Eustress: results when the energy created by stress is used beneficially.

V. INDIVIDUAL FACTORS INFLUENCING SENSITIVITY TO STRESSORS
   A. Stress Tolerance: the amount of exposure to stressors that you can tolerate before you experience stress. Varies.
   B. Biological Factors: some people have a more "excitable" autonomic nervous system than others, and are easily stressed.
   C. Personality: some characteristics lead to higher stress tolerance. Example: Kobasa's hardy personality.
   D. Past Experience With Stress: coping successfully with stress is associated with greater stress tolerance in the future.
   E. Cognitive Evaluation of the Situation: people perceive events/situations differently - usually not based entirely on "objective" facts.
   F. Life Style: smoking; drinking; eating to excess; too little sleep, exercise, or relaxation; limited social life and emotional outlets decrease stress tolerance.

VII. SITUATIONAL FACTORS INFLUENCING SENSITIVITY TO STRESSORS
   A. Nature of the stressor
   B. Number of stressors
   C. Duration of the stressor
   D. Predictablity of the stressor: stress is more severe when it is unexpected.

VIII. STRESS MANAGEMENT
   A. Effective Stress Management Goals:
      1. Find ways to adjust to stress that reduce/eliminate discomfort, and
      2. Help control future stress.
   B. Basic Alternatives for Adjusting to Stress:
      1. Change the situation
      2. Change your appraisal of the situation
      3. Change your response to the situation
      4. Escape from the situation   *
      5. Ignore the situation   *
      * do not meet the above goals
   C. Cognitive Strategies for Managing Stress: ways to control both potential and experienced stress through the way you think about the situation and by your self-talk.
      1. Evaluating the situation - think before you act, avoid oversimplification.
      2. Counter irrational self-talk - avoid catastrophizing, counter every irrational thought with a rational thought.
      3. Making positive coping self-statements - see Meichenbaum Exhibit 12-3 in the text.
   D. Behavioral Strategies for Managing Stress:

156 BASIC SKILLS FOR MORE EFFECTIVE BEHAVIOR

1. Exercise: increases energy, decreases fatigue, makes you look good, has a positive effect on your life style, has long-term health benefits
2. Time management:
    a. Identify and eliminate time wasters
    b. Identify and eliminate strategic errors in time use
    c. Plan your time
3. Assertiveness: behavior that allows you to express your personal opinions and/or feelings or helps you accomplish your goals in spite of the disagreement or opposition of others. The power lies in the sense of control you feel. This is not to be confused with aggressiveness. Difficulties in becoming assertive:
    a. Socialized to be respectful and polite to others
    b. Often violates a social norm
    c. Fear
4. Strong social support network*
5. Adequate financial resources*
6. Activity*
7. Biofeedback, meditation, systematic desensitization*

* not discussed in detail in the text

REVIEW QUESTIONS

MATCHING: Match the words and phrases below with the definitions

a. stress
b. adapted state
c. daily hassles
d. frustration
e. pressure

f. resistance stage of G.A.S.
g. exhaustion stage of G.A.S.
h. alarm stage of G.A.S.
i. stressor
j. psychophysiological problems

1. _a_ A significant departure from an individual adapted state.
2. _b_ Your usual state as your life runs along day-to-day.
3. _c_ Traffic jams, lost keys, a long wait at the check-out counter.
4. _d_ The blocking of goal directed behavior
5. _j_ Health problems which are brought on by or increased by stress.
6. _h_ Your body is alerted to action, fight or flight.
7. _e_ Perceived psychological stressor that you must change, speed up, accomplish, or finish something.
8. _f_ The time when you and your body try to adapt to a new state of affairs.
9. _i_ Events and situations which create stress
10. _g_ When your body can no longer fight the stressor.

PEOPLE YOU SHOULD KNOW

Selye
Kobasa

Freud
Meichenbaum

STRESS AND STRESS MANAGEMENT 157

FILL-IN QUESTIONS

1. A recent view of stress is that it is not merely a stimulus or a reaction, but a _relationship_ between an individual and what is happening in his or her environment.

2. Events and conditions that have the potential to create those departures from the adapted state that we call stress are _stressors_.

3. _Frustration_ is the blocking of goal directed behavior.

4. Selye's studies of the physical changes that accompany stress led him to the conclusion that these changes follow a particular and common pattern which he called the _GAS_.

5. _Displacement_ is channeling the emotional energy created by stress into a positive activity.

6. The central fact to remember about stress is that it creates _energy_.

7. Positive responses to stress are called _eustress_.

8. Research also tells us stress is more severe when a stressor is _unexpected_ than when we know it is coming.

9. The one resource we all have the same amount of is _time_.

10. _Assertive_ behavior is behavior that allows you to express your personal opinions or feelings.

11. Whether good or bad, _change_ can create stress.

12. Protecting yourself from the perception of internal stressors by suppressing them from consciousness is called _repression_.

13. According to Kelly, a useful tool in assessing a situation rationally when you feel under stress is to train yourself to avoid _oversimplification_.

TRUE-FALSE QUESTIONS

(T) F 1. A change in your environment can cause a general stress reaction.

T (F) 2. Anticipated changes, unlike unexpected events, cannot cause stress.

TRUE F 3. The intense interest people have in the subject of stress has come about only in the past decade or so.

158 BASIC SKILLS FOR MORE EFFECTIVE BEHAVIOR

(T) F 4. There is currently no universally accepted definition of stress.

(T) F 5. Stress can be caused by positive as well as negative events in a person's life.

T (F) 6. According to Selye, an individual's G.A.S. response will vary depending on the cause of the stress.

T F 7. [FALSE] The General Adaptation Syndrome involves substantial physical and psychological changes that are caused by stress.

T F 8. [TRUE] Most psychologists believe that defense mechanisms are not healthy in the long run, but can serve as temporary checks on anxiety in the short run.

(T) F 9. [TRUE] Defense mechanisms were considered by Freud to be abnormal responses to stress.

(T) F 10. Unlike many defense mechanisms, displacement and ventilation are considered to be positive coping mechanisms for dealing with stress.

(T) F 11. Distress refers to a negative response to stress while eustress refers to a positive response to stress.

(T) F 12. Extremely stressful events that occur early in life seem to have long-lasting negative effects on stress tolerance.

T (F) 13. [FALSE] Cognitive strategies for managing stress include ways to change the situation and/or your response to the situation.

T (F) 14. Countering every irrational thought with one that is rational is called catastrophizing.

(T) F 15. When it comes to managing stress, the power of assertiveness lies in the control it gives the individual over stressful situations.

T (F) 16. Stress is always bad and should be avoided as much as possible in order to remain healthy and happy.

(T) F 17. Stress can make a person susceptible to asthma, alergies, headaches and even cancer.

(T) F 18. Assertiveness is difficult for many of us to master due to the way in which we have been socialized.

MULTIPLE-CHOICE QUESTIONS

STRESS AND STRESS MANAGEMENT   159

1. Which of the following is NOT a view of stress discussed in the text. Stress is seen as:
   a. a reaction to a stimulus event
   b. an expected and constant reaction to certain stimuli
   c. the stimulus itself
   d. the relationship between an individual and a stimulus

2. According to the text, stress may be defined as a significant departure from:
   a. pleasant daily activities or events
   b. the G.A.S.
   c. an individual adapted state
   d. common reactions to events

3. Which of the following events would NOT cause stress?
   a. getting married
   b. the death of a spouse
   c. getting divorced
   d. all could create stress

4. A stressor is often perceived to be more stressful if it is:
   a. positive but overwhelming
   b. negative and expected/dreaded
   c. negative and beyond control
   d. negative but controllable

5. Frustration creates tension which can be a stressor. Which of the following is NOT a precurser to frustration mentioned in the text?
   a. being too shy
   b. the general stress reaction
   c. the inability to find something
   d. pushing yourself too hard

6. Which of the following is the most important qualifier when speaking about a person's reaction to pressure?
   a. perceived
   b. amount
   c. expected
   d. unexpected

7. Which of the following is NOT one of Selye's three stages of G.A.S.
   a. resistance
   b. exhaustion
   c. alarm
   d. frustration

8. In which stage of Selye's G.A.S. would you expect to experience "fight or flight" feelings?
   a. resistance
   b. exhaustion
   c. alarm

160 BASIC SKILLS FOR MORE EFFECTIVE BEHAVIOR

      d. frustration

9. Psychological responses which cushion the blow when we experience stress are called:
    a. psychosomatic reactions
    (b.) defense mechanisms
    c. adaptation reactions
    d. psychophysiological reactions

10. The study of the relationship between behavior and health is called:
    a. psychophysiology
    b. behaviorism
    (c.) behavioral immunology
    d. bio-immunology

11. If, after breaking up with your boyfriend or girlfriend, you spent two hours on the phone with your best friend, complaining, crying, and generally letting off steam, it could be said that you were using the coping mechanism of:
    a. projection
    b. anger
    c. displacement
    (d.) ventilation

12. Which of the following is NOT considered to be a defense mechanism?
    a. regression
    b. fantasizing
    c. intellectualization
    (d.) reactive inhibition

13. Distress and eustress both create:
    a. excitement
    (b.) energy
    c. fear
    d. exhaustion

14. The fact that you can study while the t.v. and/or sterio is turned on, but your room-mate must have complete silence in order to concentrate is an example of different levels of:
    (a.) stress tolerance
    b. displacement
    c. frustration
    d. pressure

15. Which of the following characteristics is NOT an example of Kobasa's hardy personality described in your text? The person:
    a. has a strong sense of commitment to a goal
    b. places greater value on challenge than on security
    (c.) believes that good luck will prevail
    d. has an internal locus of control

STRESS AND STRESS MANAGEMENT   161

16. Which of the following will DECREASE your ability to successfully cope with stress?
    a. having limited social relationships
    b. getting too little sleep
    c. smoking, drinking, or eating to excess
    (d.) all of the above

17. Which of the following is NOT a situational factor influencing sensitivity to stressors mentioned in your text?
    a. number of stressors
    (b.) displacement of the stressor
    c. nature of the stressor
    d. duration of the stressor

18. Finding effective ways to adjust to stress that reduce/eliminate discomfort when it occurs and help to control the amount of stress you experience in the future is called:
    a. an evaluation process
    b. a defense mechanism
    (c.) stress management
    d. catastrophizing

19. According to Meichenbaum, you can lower the physiological arousal level associated with stress by:
    a. deep breathing exercises
    b. regular exercize
    c. using a defense mechanism until you are able to cope with the situation (but no longer)
    (d.) rational self-talk

20. According to your text, which of the following is NOT a potential outcome of regular exercise?
    a. the need to exercise can become a stressor
    b. exercise makes you look better
    c. exercise decreases fatigue
    (d.) all of the above are potential outcomes of exercise

21. One way in which a person might decrease the level of stress in their life is by developing better _____ management skills.
    (a.) time
    b. strategic
    c. eustress
    d. cognitive

22. Which of the following is NOT identified in your text as a step to control time more wisely?
    a. identify time wasters
    b. eliminate strategic errors in time use
    (c.) eliminate "to do" lists
    d. plan your time

162 BASIC SKILLS FOR MORE EFFECTIVE BEHAVIOR

23. "If you want something done right, do it yourself" is an example of:
    a. oversimplification
    b. counterproductive assumption
    c. resistance
    d. wise planning

24. What kind of behavior allows you to express your personal opinions or feelings or helps you accomplish your goals in spite of disagreement or opposition of others. It puts you in control.
    a. aggressiveness
    b. assertiveness
    c. hostility
    d. management

PEOPLE: HOW MUCH DO YOU KNOW?

Write what you can about the people listed below (as it relates to what you learned in this chapter).

Selye   GAS

Freud

Kobasa
      HARDY PERSONALITY

Meichenbaum

STRESS AND STRESS MANAGEMENT   163

PERSONAL GROWTH EXERCISE - YOUR REACTIONS TO STRESS

Purpose: To examine your previous reactions to stress and to identify strategies that may be useful in dealing with future stress.

Step One: Identify a significant stressful situation that has occurred fairly recently in your life:

Step Two: Analyze the situation by filling in the blanks after each of the following items:

a. What was the nature of the stressor?

        Positive _____ or Negative _____

        Long Duration _____ or Short Duration _____

        Environmental _____ or Psychological _____

        Predictable _____ or Unexpected _____

        By Itself _____ or One of Many _____

b. What was your reaction to the stressor?

    Physical _____. If so, analyze your reaction using the three stages (alarm, resistance, and exhaustion) in Selye's General Adaptation Syndrome.

    Psychological _____. If so, was it caused more by:

        Frustration _____ or Pressure _____

    Which of the following reactions did you employ in order to cope with the situation? (Be honest!)

Denial ____	Repression ____	Projection ____
Displacement ____	Fantasizing ____	Ventilation ____
Anger ____	Regression ____	Intellectualizing ____
Alcohol ____	Tranquilizers ____	Street Drugs ____

Other (describe):

164 BASIC SKILLS FOR MORE EFFECTIVE BEHAVIOR

Step Three: Analyze your reaction

In retrospect, are you satisfied with the way in which your handled the stressor?

  Yes _____ (well done!)   No _____

If no, which of the following strategies do you feel might be most useful to you in dealing with your next stressful situation more successfully? (Check as many as you deem appropriate)

- Evaluate the situation before acting ____
- Control irrational self-talk ____
- Make positive coping self-statements ____
- Stay physically fit (exercise) ____
- Maintain a healthy diet ____
- Time management ____
- Assertiveness ____
- Use a social support network ____
- Adequate financial resources/planning ____
- Increased activity (work, sports, social activity, volunteerism ____
- Biofeedback ____
- Meditation ____
- Systematic desensitization ____

Step Four: Keep a Stress Diary. Detail stressful events and situations and how you handled each experience. This will not only help you to evaluate your coping techniques, but it will also be a record of past experiences which you have survived. This will help you to be more optimistic when faced with future stressors.

STRESS AND STRESS MANAGEMENT 165

PERSONAL GROWTH EXERCISE - THE EFFECTS OF STRESS

A. List the negative effects of stress:

      Psychological   Physical

B. List the positive effects of stress:

      Psychological   Physical

C. List ways in which you can reduce the negative effects of stress in your life:

      Psychological   Physical

D. List ways in which you can increase the positive effects of stress in your life:

      Psychological   Physical

PERSONAL GROWTH EXERCISE - SHYNESS

Purpose: To determine whether or not you might suffer from shyness in social situations, and to identify strategies which have proved to be successful in reducing shyness in other people.

Answer the following questions:

1. Do you always feel uncomfortable in unfamiliar social situations?
2. Do you find it difficult to talk with strangers?
3. Would you almost prefer physical torture to having to speak in front of an audience?
4. Do you feel awkward around members of the opposite sex, particularly if, in a mixed-sex group, you are attracted to someone in the group?
5. If you attend a party where you know only one or two people, do you panic when they are not around you and you have to fend for yourself?
6. Do you find yourself not speaking up in class even when you think that you have something relevant to say?
7. Are you terrified of walking into a room full of strangers?

If you answer "yes" to all or any of the above questions, you probably suffer from some degree of shyness. Shyness can range from the very mild case in certain situations to severe cases which become debilitating for some people.

Shyness can be cured! However, it does take a conscious effort to overcome those terrible feelings of fear, anxiety, apprehension, nervousness, and even nausea which often lead people to avoid certain situations.

Steps to Reduce Shyness

1. Learn to relax - you might try deep breathing exercises, or you may need to use other relaxation methods. There are several good tapes available (in most book stores) which will teach you how to relax.
2. Feel good about yourself - you are a worthwhile person, and you do have something interesting to say.
3. Make a list of your good qualities and talents and accentuate them.
4. If you feel that you have some negative characteristics, work on trying to eliminate or soften them. Remember that no-one is perfect!
5. Ask a trusted friend to help you to role-play certain social situations prior to the actual event. Don't be embarrassed - this could help him or her as much as it helps you.

6. During a conversation, try to ask open-ended questions (questions which cannot be answered by a simple "yes" or "no"). At the same time, try to avoid giving "yes" or "no" or "fine" answers if you want the conversation to continue. When someone keeps receiving one-word answers to his or her enquiries they soon become tired or bored and move on.

7. Be interested. If you want to impress someone, listen to them - really listen! Most people like to talk about themselves, their hobbies, their job, the course they are taking, etc. If you want to get to know someone better, find out what their pet subject of the day is, and let them know that you are eager to listen and learn. (Use the active listening techniques discussed in your text.)

8. Smile. Even if you are feeling lost and lonely - smile. Think of something that you enjoy doing and smile, with both your mouth and your eyes. This will not only relax the tension in your face and neck, but it will also make you look more attractive and more approachable.

9. Try not to view every social situation as a battle (me against them). Remember that the other people around you are not monsters who are waiting for you to say or do something foolish. In fact, many of them are probably shy too, so again - relax!

PERSONAL GROWTH EXERCISE - TIME MANAGEMENT SKILLS

Purpose: To determine how organized you are, identify time wasters, and evaluate your need for increasing your time management skills.

In the past two months have you:

Situation	3 or more times	twice	once	never
Been late for class	+2	+1	-1	-2
Missed class (too late to go in)	+2	+1	-1	-2
Been late for work	+2	+1	-1	-2
Missed work (too late to go)	+2	+1	-1	-2
Had trouble deciding what to wear	+2	+	-1	-2
Had no clean laundry	+2	+1	-1	-2
Had a very messy room/apartment	+2	+1	-1	-2
Studied for a major exam the night before	+2	+1	-1	-2
Exercised regularly	+2	+1	-1	-2
Lost your car keys	+2	+1	-1	-2
Totally recopied your own notes from class	+2	+1	-1	-2
Spent more than 10 minutes worrying about a single event/circumstance/problem	+2	+1	-1	-2
Spent longer than 60 minutes getting ready for a date/event (including shower & shampoo)	+2	+1	-1	-2
Refused to allow someone to help with a task	+2	+1	-1	-2
Done something with a friend when you had planned to use that time more constructively	+2	+1	-1	-2
Had to order a pizza-to-go because you have not had time to grocery shop	+2	+1	-1	-2
Watched a t.v. show just because the t.v. was left on after your favorite show ended	+2	+1	-1	-2
Driven to one or several stores to find something when a phone call would suffice	+2	+1	-1	-2
TOTALS				

Add the columns, and then deduct the plus columns from the minus columns. You should now have one figure which will either be a plus-figure or a minus-figure.

If your final figure is a plus-figure, you would benefit from time management skills outlined in your text.

Review: 1. Identify and eliminate time wasters
2. Identify and eliminate strategic errors
3. Plan your time - using a time budget or a "to do" list

Additional Suggestions:

Make use of small amounts of time: if you have a dentist or doctor's appointment, take along a book to read or class notes to study so that you do not waste time while you are in the waiting room.

Be flexible: don't panic when you must deviate from your daily plan.

Pay attention to your natural biorhythms: most people have certain times of the day when they seem to work better and are more alert. Get to know when you able to function at your peak of performance and plan your major activities accordingly.

Plan at least one pleasant activity each day. It does not have to be exotic or elaborate, nor even very time consuming. Just arrange to do something each day which will help you to relax and renew your energy.

CHAPTER 13
Behavior-Management Problems

LEARNING OBJECTIVES

1. Define addiction and identify the most common addictive substances in use today.

2. Understand the facts about alcoholism, its causes and cures.

3. Recognize drug abuse before it becomes out of control.

4. Understand the most common weight control problems, and why society demands that all women wear a size 8.

CHAPTER OUTLINE

I. THE USE OF ADDICTIVE SUBSTANCES
    A. Definition of Addiction: devotion to a behavior to such an extent that breaking it causes physical symptoms (physical addiction) and/or stress, discomfort, or anxiety (psychological addiction)
    B. Addictive substance: any substance with the potential for creating physical or psychological addiction
    C. Tobacco
        1. About three-quarters of all Americans have never smoked or have stopped smoking cigarettes
        2. Over 50 million people still smoke
        3. 1984: 600 billion cigarettes were sold in America
        4. 90% of all studies since the 1950s confirm:
            a. Smokers have a higher risk of lung cancer, heart disease, bronchitis, pneumonia, emphasema
            b. 340,000 smokers a year die prematurely in America
            c. Smoking affects many organs and functions in the body

5. Tobacco contains:
   a. Nicotine: one of the deadliest poisons known to man
   b. Tars: similar to those used to build roads and well-known cancer-producing agents (carcinogens)
   c. Carbon monoxide: can kill in concentrated dosages
6. Cigars, pipes, and tobacco plugs: may reduce some health risks but increase the risk of cancer of the mouth and throat

D. Why People Smoke
  1. New Smokers? About 5,000 per day, mostly under 20 years of age
  2. Imitation, advertising, and a desire to appear grown-up lead many young people to smoking
  3. Relaxation: at high levels nicotine triggers the release of betaendorphine (natural opiates) and epinephrine (a hormone) which increases the pulse rate and sends extra sugar into the blood stream. Result: a brief spurt of energy, but eventually fatigue
  4. Everybody does it! Not true any more
  5. I can't quit. Withdrawal symptoms of fatigue, headaches, insomnia, nervousness, heart palpitations, and constipation may be felt by a person initially when they try to break their addiction
  6. Nicotine: affects brain wave functioning, alters mood and serves as a biological reinforcement for behavior (three of the major criteria for calling a substance physically addictive)

E. Kicking the Habit
  1. I'll never start program: begins in 3rd grade, prevention is the best method of control
  2. Anyone can quit smoking program
  3. Nicotine gum (available by prescription) helps some people break the behavioral habits associated with smoking
  4. Stop smoking seminars are successful for many
  5. Behavior modification programs may be carried out without professional help
  6. Every cigarette counts, so cutting down is sometimes better than nothing

F. Caffeine
  1. Americans consume more caffeine than other nations, mostly in the form of coffee, tea, soft drinks, chocolate
  2. Caffeine is a powerful central nervous system stimulant
  3. Possible physical effects:
     a. Heart palpitations and irregular breathing
     b. Heart disease
     c. Gastrointestinal problems
     d. Insomnia
     e. Aggravation of anemia and fibrocystic breast disease
     f. Anxiety, depression, and panic attacks seem to increase when caffeine is consumed

G. Alcohol

1. The single most abused substance in our society
2. Alcohol is a powerful central nervous system depressant
3. Partying implies stimulation and this is the <u>initial</u> effect of alcohol on most people
4. Blood alcohol concentration: measure of alcohol in the bloodstream
   a. 0.1.10% or greater: legal intoxication
   b. .05% : you will pass out
   c. .55% : you will probably die
5. Immediate effects:
   a. Reduced muscular coordination
   b. Impaired vision and speech
   c. Impaired sexual functioning in men
   d. Memory lapses
6. After effects:
   a. Headaches
   b. Nausea
   c. Fatigue
7. Long-term effects:
   a. Nutritional deficiencies
   b. Reduced ability to fight off disease
   c. Cirrhosis (destruction) of the liver
   d. Redness of the face
   e. Enlarged veins on the nose
8. Behavioral effects:
   a. Murders: 60% are committed by intoxicated persons
   b. Rape, assault, child abuse: intoxication involved in most cases
9. Psychological effects:
   a. Lowered self-esteem
   b. Delerium tremens: disorientation, hallucination, acute fear, tremors
   c. Korsakoff's psychosis: memory impairment, lowered moral and ethical standards, reduced intellectual functioning, elaborate lying to conceal memory gaps. As result of longstanding dietary deficiencies
10. Possible positive effects of <u>moderate</u> alcohol consumption:
    a. Improves appetite
    b. Might lower the risk of heart attack

H. Who Are the Alcoholics?
   1. The definitions of "alcoholic" vary:
      a. W.H.O.: anyone who has life problems due to alcohol
      b. N.C.A.: persons exhibiting certain defined symptoms
      c. A.P.A.: persons who fit 3 or more certain defined criteria
   2. 10-15 million adult Americans have a "drinking problem"
   3. All socio-economic levels are represented
   4. 500,000 children (10-19 years of age) abuse alcohol

I. What Causes Alcohol Abuse?
   1. No single cause: biological, psychological and social factors all play a part

2. Biological: a possible genetic predisposition
3. Psychological:
   a. "the alcoholic personality" - immature, expects too much of the world, requires more praise and appreciation, low frustration tolerance, inadequate and unsure, reacts to failure badly, or
   b. Has a lowered tolerance for tension or stress and experiences high levels of both in life
   c. Alcohol becomes a self-reinforcing pattern of behavior
4. Social: cross-cultural studies show that a society's attitude toward drinking is a contributing factor

J. Coping With Alcohol Abuse
   1. Alcoholics Anonymous (A.A.): ex-alcoholics helping other alcoholics to stop drinking by support, understanding, shared techniques, the "buddy system" and example. Spiritual development is important
   2. Aversion therapy: pairs alcohol use with an unpleasant stimulus (for example: nausea or an electric shock). Basic principles of classical conditioning are utilized
   3. Antabuse: the drug used in a type of aversion therapy, makes the user seriously ill if alcohol is consumed
   4. Psychotherapy: provides non-drinking solutions to daily problems and stresses. Group therapy is preferred, and success rates vary according to:
      a. Motivation and self-esteem
      b. How long the problem has existed
      c. Severity
      d. Understanding of the problem
      e. Environment of the abuser

K. The Other Side of the Coin
   1. Many users of alcohol are not abusers
   2. People who choose not to drink need to be assertive in refusing alcohol
   3. Al-Anon: a support group for people who must deal with alcoholics (family, friends)

L. Other Drugs - Illegal and Controlled Substances
   1. 225,000 heroin addicts in the U.S. (estimated)
   2. Teenage addiction may be on the decline but adult abusers increasing

M. Why Do People Take Drugs?
   1. To change the way they feel
   2. When the drug wears off the pain, inhibition, boredom,etc. returns
   3. Many people then increase the number or size of dose
   4. Psychological addiction: a mental and emotional dependence on the altered state produced by a drug. This is the most serious kind of addiction
   5. Physical addiction: the person's body must have the drug in order to function normally. Only two major catagories of drugs (heroin and barbituates) have the potential for

BEHAVIOR MANAGEMENT PROBLEMS 175

        physical addiction
- a. Barbituates: withdrawal effects can be life-threatening, and the overdose risk is very high due to the fact that the dose needed to be effective increases far more rapidly than the body's tolerance for the drug
- N. Cocaine: The "In" Drug:
    1. A processed plant product
    2. A major drug problem today, a "glamour drug"
    3. Gives a false feeling of confidence or euphoria
    4. 25 million users (estimated) smoked or snorted
    5. Death rates for usage are increasing
    6. Clearly an addictive substance
    7. Crack is readily available in most neighborhoods
- O. Marijuana
    1. A dried plant product
    2. The drug of the 60s and 70s
    3. Joints or reefers are smoked as cigarettes, the drug may also be cooked in food (brownies)
    4. Gives a feeling of relaxation
    5. Little criminal activity or violence associated with the "grass subculture"
- P. Recognizing Drug Abuse
    1. Often difficult to differentiate
    2. A sudden onset of symptoms and a marked departure from previous behavior are things to watch for
    3. Many abusers will not admit a problem
    4. Try to obtain professional help
- Q. Over the Counter Drugs
    1. All drugs may have side effects
    2. No drug is harmless

II. EATING AND WEIGHT CONTROL
- A. The fattening of America
    1. 1 in 5 adults are overweight by 20% or more
    2. 11 million are 40% or more overweight
    3. Numbers have increased dramatically in the last 30 years
    4. Desirable weight standards have been revised consistently downward
    5. Recent analyses show higher weight recommendations
    6. Ideal Weight?
        - a. Females: 100 lbs. per 5 ft. and add 5 lbs. for each additional inch over five feet
        - b. Males: 110 lbs. per 5 ft. and add 5 lbs. for each additional inch over five feet
        - c. Ideal weight has nothing to do with your appearance but is based on physical and physiological considerations
- B. Why Are We Overweight?
    1. What we eat: healthy foods or fatty, high calorie foods?

2. When we eat: on the run, snacking
3. How we live: exercise or couch potato?
4. How much we eat: less important
C. Eat It Today--Wear It Tomorrow: Dieting and Weight Control
1. Dieting: reducing food intake and/or excluding certain foods
2. Recommended diets: the New Canadian High Energy Diet, Weight Watchers, the U.C.L.A. Diet (California Slim)
3. 3,500 excess calories means 1 lb. gained (either eat fewer calories or burn up more calories)
4. Basal Metabolic Rate (MBR): the rate at which your body expends energy (burns calories)
   a. An average sized adult requires 1400 calories per day
5. Set point: a hypothetical weight that you body is programmed to "defend"
D. Use It and Lose It: Exercise and Weight Control
1. Eat less and you will lose weight: but your body will begin adjusting to the lower intake (reduced BMR)
2. Energy budget: eat less but exercise more
3. Burn off an extra 100 calories a day: will result in a loss of 10 lbs. a year (with no dietary changes)
4. Regular exercise lowers the body's set-point
E. Should You Lose Weight?
1. Some health risks of obesity:
   a. Gout
   b. Diabetes
   c. Gallstones
   d. High blood pressure, clots and strokes
   e. Heart pain, attacks, and failure
   f. Cancer of the uterus, breast, prostate and colon
2. Other risks:
   a. Ridicule
   b. Avoided or exploited socially
   c. Excluded from activities
   d. Fewer clothes choices
3. Most people who diet and worry about their weight are not obese (most are 5-7 lbs. over the weight they want to be)
4. Plumpness: a word used to praise feminine beauty historically
5. Stoutness: in a man, a hallmark of success and prosperity historically
6. "A few extra pounds": top fashion models are now no longer super thin
F. Eating Disorders
1. Anorexia nervosa:
   a. Obssesion with being thin to the point of starvation
   b. Includes a distorted body image
   c. 1% of the female population between 12 and 25
   d. Occurs in males but is rare
   e. Complications: malnutrition, dehydration, pneumonia, death

BEHAVIOR MANAGEMENT PROBLEMS 177

   2. Bulimia:
      a. Four times as common as anorexia
      b. Large quantities of food are consumed and then vomiting is induced and/or laxatives are taken
      c. Seldom fatal
      d. Problems: digestive and dental, guilt feelings lead to anxiety and depression
   3. Professional help is usually necessary for these disorders

REVIEW QUESTIONS

MATCHING: Match the words and phrases below with the definitions

a. addiction
b. antabuse
c. basal metabolic rate
d. bulimia
e. caffeine
f. controlled substance
g. intoxication
h. nicotine
i. alcohol
j. cocaine

1. _a_ Devotion to a behavior to such an extent that breaking it causes physical symptoms and/or stress, discomfort or anxiety.
2. _h_ One of the deadliest poisons known to medical science.
3. _e_ America leads the world in its consumption of this drug.
4. _i_ The single most abused substance in our society.
5. _b_ An aversive stimulus to control one kind of drug abuse.
6. _f_ Legally obtained only by prescription.
7. _g_ Blood alcohol concentration of .10% or greater.
8. _j_ A dangerous processed plant product which is considered to be the major drug problem at this time.
9. _c_ The rate at which your body burns calories.
10. _d_ Large quantities of food are consumed and then vomiting is self-induced.

FILL-IN QUESTIONS

1. _addiction_ means being devoted to a behavior to such an extent that it causes physical symptoms and/or stress, discomfort or anxiety when forced to give up the behavior.

2. _NICOTINE_ triggers the release of natural opiates (betaendorphins) and epinephrine into the body.

3. When your _blood alcohol concentration_ reaches .05% you will pass out; when it reached .55% you will probably die.

4. It is estimated that _60%_ percent of the murders in this country are committed by intoxicated persons.

178 PROBLEMS THAT BLOCK EFFECTIVE BEHAVIOR

5. _Korsakoff psychosis_ is a psychotic reaction to prolonged alcohol abuse, characterized by memory impairment and reduced intellectual functioning.

6. The drug most widely used in aversion therapy which when combined with alcohol makes the person seriously ill is called _antabuse_.

7. _Barbiturates_ are the most dangerous drugs from the standpoint of overdose risk.

8. Long-term use of _MARIJUANA_ has been linked to lung cancer, heart problems, brain damage, a decrease in male sex hormones, and a decrease in the body's ability to fight disease.

9. The hypothetical weight that your body is programmed to defend is called _set POINT_.

10. _Basal metabolic rate BMR_ is the rate at which your body burns calories/expends energy.

11. Using tobacco in forms such as pipe, cigars, and chewing, may increase the risk of cancer of the _mouth & throat_.

12. Milk chocolate, Excedrin, and many soft drinks all contain _caffeine_.

13. The physical effects of alcohol abuse can have serious repercussions for the abuser, but there are also serious _BEHAVIORAL_ effects which must be dealt with by other people.

14. A _drug_ is any substance that alters normal functioning when taken into the body.

15. _Cocaine_, a plant product, provides a feeling of confidence and euphoria.

16. _MARIJUANA_ is far and away the single most used of the drugs that are illegal in this country.

17. The long-range effect of persistent dieting is that it simply adjusts the _BMR_ downward.

18. People who suffer from _anorexia NERVOSA_ starve themselves because they have a distorted body image.

TRUE-FALSE QUESTIONS

(T) F 1. An addictive substance is any substance that has the potential for creating physical or psychological addiction.

(T) F 2. Tobacco, alcohol and caffeine are all addictive substances.

BEHAVIOR MANAGEMENT PROBLEMS 179

(T) F 3. Smoking reduces the supply of oxygen to the brain and causes progressive hearing loss at low frequencies.

(T) F 4. Nicotine, found in cigarette smoke, is one of the deadliest poisons known to science.

T (F) 5. Smoking in public is still a socially acceptable behavior.

T (F) 6. There are some people who just can't stop smoking.

(T) F 7. Research emphasizes that every cigarette counts, so there is something to be gained from cutting down if you won't quit.

T (F) 8. Decaffeinated coffee contains no caffeine.

T (F) 9. Cocaine is the most widely abused drug in this country today.

(T) F 10. Alcohol is a powerful central nervous system depressant.

(T) F 11. If the bood alcohol concentration in your bloodsteam reaches .10% you are considered (legally) to be intoxicated.

T (F) 12. According to experts, it takes approximately ten years to become a full-fledged alcoholic.

T (F) 13. The World Health Organization defines an alcoholic as one who consumes a certain amount (specified) of alcohol each day.

(T) F 14. Children of alcohol abusers who are adopted by non-alcoholic parents have about twice the number of alcohol-related problems by their late twenties as adopted children whose natural parents had no history of alcohol abuse.

T (F) 15. Aversion therapy helps people to stop drinking by offering an alternative social environment that does not reinforce the use of alcohol.

(T) F 16. A drug addict is a person who smokes cigarettes.

(T) F 17. In general, psychological addiction is a far more serious problem than the effects of physical dependence on cocaine and heroin.

(T) F 18. The more often a person uses barbituates, the closer he or she comes to a fatal overdose because the dose needed to be effective increases far more rapidly than the body's tolerance for the drug.

T (F) 19. One of the reasons that cocaine is currently a very popular drug is because it is relatively innocuous and non-addictive.

180 PROBLEMS THAT BLOCK EFFECTIVE BEHAVIOR

(T) F 20. Marijuana is by far the single most used of the drugs that are illegal in this country today.

MULTIPLE-CHOICE QUESTIONS

1. Which of the following is NOT a finding of research regarding nicotine?
   a. affects brain wave functioning
   b. alters mood
   c. serves as a biological reinforcement for behavior
   (d.) decreases the body's tolerance for medication

2. If the blood alcohol level in your body reaches .55% you will:
   a. feel tipsy
   b. be legally intoxicated
   c. have trouble walking
   (d.) probably die

3. It is estimated that ___ percent of the murders in this country are committed by intoxicated persons.
   (a.) 60
   b. 55
   c. 47
   d. 43

4. The psychotic reaction to alcohol abuse, characterized by memory impairment, lowering of moral and ethical standards, reduced intellectual functioning, elaborate lies to fill in memory gaps and the ability to think clearly?
   a. delirium tremens
   b. antabuse
   (c.) Korsakoff's psychosis
   d. anorexia psychosis

5. Legal intoxication involves a minimum blood alcohol level of ___ percent or higher.
   a. .001
   b. .01
   (c.) .1
   d. .55

6. Which of the following is NOT true of alcohol?
   a. alcohol is a depressant
   (b.) the physiological withdrawal from alcohol is not dangerous
   c. exercise will not speed up the process of getting alcohol from your system
   d. black coffee will not counteract the negative effects of alcohol

7. Those people who believe there is an "alcoholic personality" would

be subscribing to which theory of alcohol abuse?
a. physiological
b. psychological ✓
c. biological
d. sociological

8. Which method of coping with alcohol abuse offers an alternative social environment that does not reinforce the use of alcohol for the user?
   a. aversion therapy
   b. antabuse therapy
   c. psychotherapy
   d. A.A. ✓

9. A controlled substance is a drug which is:
   a. an over-the-counter drug
   b. an illegal substance
   c. legally obtained only by prescription ✓
   d. cocaine, heroin, LSD

10. Most people take drugs to:
    a. change the way they feel ✓
    b. become a free spirit
    c. fit in with the crowd
    d. overcome boredom

11. What are the only major catagories of drugs which have been proved to have the potential for physical addiction?
    a. amphetamines and barbituates
    b. cocaine and heroin
    c. heroin and LSD
    d. heroin and barbituates ✓

12. Withdrawal effects from this catagory of drugs may be life threatening.
    a. heroin
    b. barbituates ✓
    c. cocaine
    d. acid

13. What is the single most used illegal drug in this country today?
    a. cocaine
    b. alcohol
    c. marijuana ✓
    d. speed

14. Which of the following drugs could have serious negative side effects?
    a. aspirin
    b. laxatives
    c. barbituates

d. all of the above *(circled)*

15. If you are a male who is 6 ft. fall, your ideal weight would be (as detailed in your text):
    a. 160 lbs
    b. 170 lbs *(circled)*
    c. 175 lbs
    d. 180 lbs

16. The eating disorder in which starvation plays a role is called:
    a. yo-yo dieting
    b. bulimia
    c. anorexia *(circled)*
    d. obsessive bulimia

PERSONAL GROWTH EXERCISE - ALCOHOL ABUSE

PURPOSE   To determine your risk for alcohol abuse.

1. How did you learn about alcohol?

    a. from parents who showed consistent examples of either moderation or abstinence

    b. from friends

    c. from alcoholic parent or close relative

2. How do you feel about drinking?

    a. I admire people who can hold their liquor

    b. drinking is not associated with strength or adulthood

3. Your social group accepts drinking in excess

    a. often

    b. rarely

4. Alcohol is only taken with meals

    a. usually

    b. alcohol is taken any time and often

5. Do you ever drive after drinking?

    a. never

    b. sometimes

6. Would you describe yourself as an extrovert, impulsive, a rule breaker?

    a. yes

    b. no

SCORE: b   b   b   a   a   b

Give yourself 1 point for each of the above

There are no points for other answers

For each point below 6 your risk for alcohol abuse increases

PERSONAL GROWTH EXERCISE - ADDICTIONS

PURSOSE___ To determine whether or not you are addicted to any substances.

1. Do you use tobacco in any form:

    cigarettes _____   pipe _____   chew _____

2. Do you drink:

    coffee _____   tea _____   chocolate

3. Are you a "chocoholic"

    Yes _____   No _____

4. Do you drink:

    liquor _____   wine _____   beer _____

5. Have you ever smoked marijuana

    Yes _____   No _____

6. Have you ever used:

    amphetamines

    barbituates

    cocaine

    heroin

    LSD

    PCP

7. Do you consider yourself addicted to any of the above drugs?

    Yes _____   No _____

8. If yes, you might want to try to break your addiction. Use the behavior modification technique described in Appendix A of your text:
    a. Chart the behavior
    b. Chart the situation
    c. Break the links
    d. Set up intermediate goals
    e. Reward yourself for successful goal accomplishments

CHAPTER 14
Relationship Problems

LEARNING OBJECTIVES

1. List and define the problems we have getting along with other people in our social world.

2. Understand peer pressure and the influence it can have on behavior.

3. Identify the most common problems associated with special relationships.

4. Detail the special problems encountered when a marriage ends.

CHAPTER OUTLINE

I. PROBLEMS GETTING ALONG IN THE WORLD
   A. Self-consciousness
      1. Three types as defined by Fenigster, Scheier, and Buss(1975)
         a. Public self-consciousness: being overly aware of how we appear to others, concerned with the "right" clothes and behavior, the assumption that virtually all situations are relevant to themselves
         b. Private self-consciousness: concentration on one's own feelings and thoughts, introspection, more satisfying intimate relationships
         c. Social self-consciousness: generalized anxiety in the presence of others, easily embarrassed, avoid scenes, poor self-esteem, most distressing
   B. Shyness
      1. Definition: a high degree of caution in interpersonal relationships

2. Zimbardo made an extensive study of shyness:
   a. Shyness is not a deep-rooted personality trait
   b. Most people can overcome shyness
   c. The keys: understanding the problem, building self-esteem, and improving social skills

C. Loneliness
   1. <u>Social loneliness</u>: occurs when a person does not have a network of friends and acquaintances with whom to share life
   2. <u>Situational loneliness</u>: occurs when something about a persons life circumstances is causing him or her to feel lonely
   3. <u>Emotional loneliness</u>: stems from a dearth of intimate relationships
   4. Who is more likely to be lonely?
      a. Not the elderly
      b. 18-25 age group
      c. More men than women

II. PROBLEMS WITH PEERS AND FRIENDS
   A. Peer Pressure and Influence
      1. Reference groups: the most important groups to which we belong and which influence the way we think about things and the way we evaluate our own behavior
   B. When the Group Wants Too Much
      1. Acceptance has a price tag: sometimes we are expected to do things we don't want to do, expectations for conformity
      2. Non-conformity:
         a. Groups need a certain amount to remain flexible
         b. Idiosyncratic credits: high status individuals have more credits which allow deviance (Hollander, 1964)
         c. Competence, exceptional ability, allows for non-conformity
   C. Resisting Group Influence
      1. Conform: to change your behavior or belief so that it agrees with those of some group (or grouping) of other people
      2. Who resists conformity?
         a. More intelligent people
         b. Those who hold strong personal values
         c. Those with high self-esteem
         d. Those with a strong belief in their own opinions, values, and competence
   D. The Power of Group Concensus
      1. The Asch Study of Conformity found:
         a. Group concensus has a strong influence on an individual's confidence in his or her own position
         b. It is possible to be right when everyone else is wrong
   E. When Friends Impose - How Do You Say No?
      1. Don't apologize for turning down a request

2. Don't make excuses for refusing
3. Don't blame someone else for your inability to help
4. Learn to use the phrase "not willing"
5. Say no to the request, not the friend
6. Show that you understand and sympathize with the friend's problem
7. Tell what you _are_ prepared to do
8. If you agree to do something, don't be a martyr

III. PROBLEMS WITH SPECIAL RELATIONSHIPS
    A. Looking For a Special Someone: Why Is It So Hard?
       1. I'm not good-looking enough
          a. Some people give up looking
          b. Others will not accept a partner who is equally as attractive as themselves
          c. Studies show that couples of equal attractiveness are likely to form long-lasting relationships
       2. I don't know what men/women want anymore (sex-role conflict due to transition from old sex-role stereotypes)
       3. I never meet any eligible men/women - Where to meet?
          a. 1950s: social clubs, church
          b. 1960s: back to school, join "a cause"
          c. 1970s: the bar scene
          d. 1980s: health and fitness clubs, cruises, singles resorts, "lonely hearts clubs"
    B. Relationship Killers
       1. Hostility: antagonism or unfriendliness toward the opposite sex may be:
          a. General hostility: "the war between the sexes"
          b. Displaced hostility: taking out hostility toward someone else on your partner
       2. Jealousy: an emotional experience characterized by a feeling that your relationship is being threatened in some way by a person or persons from outside
          a. May be mild agitation to uncontrollable jealous rages
          b. Often independent of any deliberate act of the partner
          c. A by-product of past experiences and insecurity, immaturity and or low self-esteem
          d. Single or cohabiting people more prone to jealousy
          e. Almost no-one claims _never_ to have been jealous
          f. Chronic jealousy: almost always destructive (the accused may actually have an affair or leave the relationship)
          g. If you are not jealous, does that mean you don't care?
       3. Lack of Trust
          a. Trust requires sufficient faith to put yourself at risk, to be open, and leave yourself vulnerable
          b. Remple, Holmes, and Zanna (1985) defined elements of trust as:
             i. dependability

            ii. predictability
           iii. faith
   C. When the Relationship is in Trouble: Shape Up Or Ship Out?
      1. Don't "wait and see"
         a. Things rarely improve all by themselves
         b. Gives a feeling of being out of control of the situation
      2. Communication in special relationships
         a. Involves the way you look, move; your voice tone, posture; your responses, and your behavior, as well as what you say
         b. Withholding information
         c. Poor timing: don't complain/argue/discuss problems in public, when tired, when there isn't enough time
         d. Not listening: causes resentment and hurt feelings. Listen to what is meant as well as what is being said
         e. Not talking: language and intimacy are interwoven
   D. Trail Separations
      1. Motivation for the "time out" is an important factor:
         a. As a first step toward leaving: you will speed up the process of leaving
         b. Both want to save the relationship: it could work
      2. Ways to increase the chances that a trial separation will help:
         a. Spend time alone if you can
         b. Don't look for someone new during the separation
         c. Avoid serious matters and try to have fun if you see your partner
         d. Set a personal goal for yourself (take a course for fun or lose five pounds)

IV. DIVORCE: THE SPECIAL PROBLEMS OF ENDING A MARRIAGE
    A. Why Do Marriages Break Up?
       1. Changes in the role of the family: the family unit is less critical today
       2. Employed wives: women are no longer economically dependent
       3. Fewer moral and religious sanctions: the right to individual happiness and fulfillment is now more important than one's "duty"
       4. Liberal divorce laws
       5. Social acceptance of divorce: a change in the climate for divorce
    B. A Multitude of Divorces
       1. Six stations of divorce (Bohannan, 1970):
          a. The Emotional Divorce: love replaced by indifference/ antagonism
          b. The Economic Divorce: lowered standard of living after the divorce
          c. The Legal Divorce: the public aspect of splitting up
          d. The Coparental Divorce: the impact of divorce on

children
        e. The Community Divorce: new social ties must be built
        f. The Psychic Divorce: becoming a whole and autonomous single person again
  C. Adjusting to Divorce
     1. No matter who institutes the proceedings, divorce is rarely easy for either partner
     2. Acceptance: differs for males and females even in similar situations
     3. Ten tips:
        a. Avoid spending time with people who encourage self-pity
        b. Avoid jumping into another relationship immediately
        c. Allow yourself to feel depressed, irritable, or impatent upon occasion
        d. Avoid constant rehashing
        e. Take good care of yourself
        f. Avoid saying negative things to your children
        g. Schedule some fun into your life
        h. Keep interactions with your ex-spouse matter-of-fact
        i. Consider getting professional help if you need it
        j. Keep alcohol consumption to a minimum

REVIEW QUESTIONS

MATCHING: Match the words and phrases below with the definitions

a. economic divorce
b. group consensus
c. idiosyncratic credits
d. introspection
e. private self-consciousness
f. public self-consciousness
g. reference group
h. shyness
i. situational loneliness
j. social loneliness

1. _f_ Being overly aware of how we appear to others, very concerned with appearance.
2. _e_ A very high level of attention to one's own feelings and thoughts.
3. _h_ Avoiding putting yourself forward and becoming anxious if put into the spotlight.
4. _j_ Comes about when a person does not have a network of friends and acquaintances with whom to share life.
5. _i_ Something about a person's life circumstances is causing a problem.
6. _d_ Consciousness of self.
7. _g_ Influence the way we think about things and the way we evaluate our own behavior and the behavior of others.
8. _c_ A license to behave in individual, nonconformist ways while maintaining participation in your group of choice.
9. _b_ Can have a strong influence on an individual's confidence in his or her own position.
10. _a_ When joint resources are not sufficient to sustain both partners and any children at the same standard of living.

192 PROBLEMS THAT BLOCK EFFECTIVE BEHAVIOR

PEOPLE YOU SHOULD KNOW

Zimbardo — shyness
Hollander
Asch
Remple, Holmes and Zanna
Bohannan

FILL-IN QUESTIONS

1. People with greater tendencies toward introspection have _more_ satisfying intimate relationships with others.

2. Zimbardo stated that the keys to overcoming shyness are: understanding the problem, building up self-esteem, and _Improving Social Skills_.

3. _situational_ loneliness occurs when something in the person's individual life circumstances is causing him or her to feel lonely.

4. _norms_ are unwritten rules for behavior that grow out of the social interaction of some group or grouping.

5. There is a relationship between _competance_ and the extent to which someone may deviate from group norms.

6. _More intelligent_ people are able to resist influence attempts more successfully than others.

7. _jealousy_ an emotional experience characterized by a feeling that your relationship is being threatened by a person or persons outside the relationship.

8. Like hostility and jealousy, lack of trust in a relationship may be _one sided_ as well as _mutual_.

9. In the Thompson study of divorce, it was found that _men_ whose friends did not disapprove of the divorce were more accepting of the situation, but friend approval or disapproval was not a significant factor for _women_.

10. _private_ self-consciousness refers to a very high level of attention to one's own feelings and thoughts.

11. _public_ self-consciousness refers to being overly aware of how we appear to others.

12. _social_ self-consciousness is a generalized anxiety in the presence of others.

RELATIONSHIP PROBLEMS 193

13. Self-conscious people who suffer from high social self-consciousness and _shy_ people have much in common.

14. _emotional_ loneliness stems from a dearth of intimate relationships.

15. _Expectations_ for conformity to groups in dress, behavior, and expressed opinions do not end when we turn 21 or when we leave school.

16. There is a relationship between _competance_ and the extent to which someone may deviate from group norms.

17. When refusing to do a favor for a friend, _"not willing"_ sounds much more objective and less emotional than won't.

18. In this age of unparalleled interaction of the sexes, freedom of personal choice, and sexual permissiveness, finding that special someone is _more difficult than ever_.

19. Three relationship killers mentioned in your text: _hostility_, _jealousy_, and _lack of trust_.

20. Social changes today may be summed up by saying there is a change in the _climate_ for divorce.

TRUE-FALSE QUESTIONS

T (F) 1. Shyness is the term used to mean being overly aware of how we appear to others.

(T) F 2. Extreme social self-consciousness has much in common with phobias.

(T) F 3. According to Zimbardo, the keys to overcoming shyness are, understanding the problem, building up self-esteem and improving social skills.

T (F) 4. Emotional loneliness is the loneliness that comes about when a person does not have a network of friends and acquaintances with whom to share life.

(T) F 5. Most groups tolerate some deviance from their expectations before you are at risk of being relegated to being an outsider.

(T) F 6. More intillegent people seem to be able to resist influence attempts from groups more successfully.

T (F) 7. Group concensus has no influence on an individual's confidence in his or her own position when the individual has strong beliefs.

194 PROBLEMS THAT BLOCK EFFECTIVE BEHAVIOR

T (F) 8. A good way to tell a friend you can't do something he wants you to do (without hurting his feelings) is to make up a believable excuse he will never discover was not true.

(T) F 9. Most people want and expect to marry, but in 1988 the percentage of the population that was single was about 40%.

(T) F 10. Jealousy often occurs independently of any deliberate act of the partner.

T (F) 11. When a relationship is in trouble, the best thing to do for a while is to sit back and wait to see what is going to happen next.

(T) F 12. A major problem in lack of communication between couples is a failure of one or both partners to listen to the other.

(T) F 13. The first reactions of children to the divorce of their parents are fear and anger.

T (F) 14. In the Thompson and Spanier study of divorce, it was found that the degree of emotional acceptance of the situation for men and for women was increased significantly if friends approved of the divorce action.

MULTIPLE-CHOICE QUESTIONS

1. Fenigstein and his associates believe there are three types of self-consciousness. Which of the following is NOT one of those types?
   a. public
   b. private
   (c.) introspective
   d. social

2. What is the term used to indicate a high degree of caution in interpersonal relationships?
   a. social self-consciousness
   b. introspection
   c. agoraphobia
   (d.) shyness

3. The loneliness that comes about when one does not have a network of friends and acquaintances with whom to share life is called:
   a. situational
   (b.) social
   c. emotional
   d. reclusive

4. If you are a member of a religious group, part of your opinions, self-evaluation of your life-style and devotion is based upon other

members of your church. What would your church group be known as?
   a. peers
   b. norm setter
   c. reference group *(circled)*
   d. major influence

5. According to Hollander, what does the group's tolerance for the amount of deviance it will accept depend upon?
   a. idiosyncratic credits *(circled)*
   b. conformity credits
   c. status
   d. leadership

6. In Asch's study, he discovered that _____ can have a strong influence on an individual's confidence in his or her own position.
   a. competance
   b. group consensus *(circled)*
   c. intelligence
   d. personal values

7. In 1988, what was the percentage of the population that was single in this country?
   a. 29
   b. 32
   c. 40 *(circled)*
   d. 43

8. According to your text, one of the following was NOT among the most common reasons given for not being able to find "that special someone to love."
   a. I'm not good looking enough
   b. I'm too fat
   c. I don't know what men want anymore
   d. I find that I feel hostile to members of the opposite sex *(circled)*

9. Jealousy is often a product of:
   a. insecurity
   b. immaturity
   c. low self-esteem
   d. all of the above *(circled)*

10. If your spouse asks, "Do you still love me?" what would be the best reply?
    a. "Of course I do"
    b. "Yes, I love you as much now as the day I married you"
    c. "I love you more now than ever"
    d. "Yes, I love you. Haven't I been showing you enough lately?" *(circled)*

11. During a trial separation what should you try to do?
    a. meet with your partner occassionally to try to iron out your problems even if it means arguments.

196 PROBLEMS THAT BLOCK EFFECTIVE BEHAVIOR

    b. be open to the possibility of someone new in your life
    c. set a goal for yourself (lose weight, learn something new)
    d. all of the above

12. According to Bohannan's six stations of divorce, which kind of divorce is the public aspect of splitting up?
    a. legal
    b. emotional
    c. community
    d. psychic

13. According to sociologists, psychologists, and others who study the problem of divorce believe that a number of factors in the social environment of this country play a role in our high divorce rate. Which of the following is NOT a factor mentioned in your text?
    a. changes in the role of the family
    b. immaturity
    c. employed wives
    d. liberal divorce laws

14. What are the most common first reactions of children to the divorce of their parents?
    a. anger
    b. sadness
    c. anger and fear
    d. all of the above

15. What should you NOT do following a divorce?
    a. allow yourself to feel depressed, irritable or impatient upon occasion
    b. schedule fun into your life
    c. keep alcohol consumption to a minimun
    d. spend time with people who will commiserate with you

PEOPLE: HOW MUCH DO YOU KNOW?

Write what you can about the people listed below (as it relates to what you learned in this chapter).

Zimbardo

Keys to overcoming shyness

Hollander

Asch
group consensus

Remple, Holmes and Zanna

Bohannan
6 stations of divorce

198 PROBLEMS THAT BLOCK EFFECTIVE BEHAVIOR

PERSONAL GROWTH EXERCISE - REFLECTIVE LISTENING

PURPOSE To test your own skills of reflective listening, and to help you to become more aware of the difference between reflective listening and surface listening.

When we want to share something with someone we all want to be understood and accepted. Often we are not understood and the listener is judgemental. In any relationship this can be a problem; in marriage and/or in dealing with our children it becomes a serious problem.

Test yourself on the responses below:

		reflective	judgemental

1. Comment: I did it. I got my raise.
   Reply: You should have asked for it sooner.
   Reply: You feel great about that.

2. Comment: I just broke the lawn mower on a big stick.
   Reply: I told you not to mow without clearing the yard first.
   Reply: You're upset because that means that you will have to spend hours fixing it.

3. Comment: I've finished my report for the committee. I hope they like it.
   Reply: I'm sure it will be just fine.
   Reply: You know you've done your best and you are nervous about presenting it before the committee.

4. Comment: I dropped a carton of eggs in the grocery store today.
   Reply: That sure was stupid.
   Reply: Sounds as if you were embarrassed.

5. Comment: I ran out of gas on the way to work.
   Reply: You should have noticed the empty tank yesterday.
   Reply: That must have been annoying for you.

6. Comment: Bobby and Jimmy ganged up on me at school today, and said that they would not be friends anymore.

Reply: You'll find other friends.   _____   _____
Reply: Sounds as if you had a bad day and are
        feeling hurt and angry.   _____   _____

You probably did not have any difficulty in choosing the best reply from the two choices, however, how many times have you <u>given</u> a reply which was judgemental and which did not acknowledge the other person's feelings?

Think of the times when you have either said or heard the phrase "Oh, you just don't understand!" When this happens between you and someone who is important to you, ask them if the two of you can sit down and try to come to a better understanding of the situation. A good way to open up the conversation might be, "I'm sorry, but I am having trouble understanding how you are feeling at this moment/exactly what you mean by that/what I can do to make this situation better. Perhaps we can sit down and you can help me to understand things from your point of view." Never be condescending. Show an honest desire to understand the other person's feelings.

200 PROBLEMS THAT BLOCK EFFECTIVE BEHAVIOR

PERSONAL GROWTH EXERCISE - COMMUNICATION IN MARRIAGE

<u>PURPOSE</u> To determine how well you and your spouse communicate, and to learn some communication tips.

1. Do you feel that you and your spouse communicate enough?

    Yes _____   No _____

2. What do you talk about?

    children _____   money _____   school _____   relatives _____

    the future _____   politics _____   religion _____   the car _____

    t.v. _____   sex _____   work _____   feelings _____

    the community _____   hopes, dreams, fantasies _____

3. What percentage of your conversations are concerned with negative topics?

    90-100% _____   80-89% _____   60-79% _____   35-59% _____

              under 35% _____

(Many women who complain that their husbands won't talk to them have a pattern of conversation which is mostly negative or problem solving. Problems cannot be ignored, but there should be a balance and a good variety in all of our conversations.)

4. When was the last time you said, "I love you?"

    Today _____   Yesterday _____   This week _____   Longer _____

5. When was the last time you complimented your mate?

    Today _____   Yesterday _____   This week _____   Longer _____

6. Do you give guests in your home more respect and consideration than you do your own family?

7. Are you waiting for your mate to become more attentive toward you before you become more attentive yourself?

    Yes _____   No _____

(Remember back to when you first started dating, would you have behaved in the same way then as you do now?)

8. Does your spouse have a responsible job?

    Yes _____   No _____

9. If yes, is there a dramatic change in the way he/she is treated at home?

    Yes _____   No _____

(Many men who divorce their wives after 15-20 years of marriage give as a major reason that their wife never acknowledged their competence; all they saw was the man who left his dirty laundry all over the bathroom, and/or the young insecure man just starting out in his new career. Today, women are voicing similar complaints as they decide on divorce as an alternative to living with a man who sees her as primarily a woman who is working "to help out financially."
We all tend to show our best face to the world, but at the same time what we want in our partner is someone who will compliment, nurture, and try to understand us. Acknowledge and admire your partner's accomplishments - even if you have to look very hard to find them! The possible benefits will be that the more you admire, the more there will be to admire.)

10. Do you think that in order to have a good marriage each partner must give a 50-50 share.

    Yes _____   No _____

(Anything less than 100% each and you are not giving enough. Relationships take total commitment if they are to work well.)

11. What could you say to your mate that you know would:

    a. make him/her angry

    b. hurt him/her

    c. make him/her happy

    d. make him/her sad

(People who are very close know all the right or wrong buttons to press in order to stir emotions. Unfortunately, it is more often the wrong buttons that get pushed.)

12. Do you believe that if you love someone you should share all thoughts and emotions?

    Yes _____   No _____

(In fact, most successful couples admit that there are a few topics which are "off-limits" for them if they are to avoid serious arguments.)

13. Do you believe that if someone loves you, he/she should know just how you are feeling without being told?

    Yes _____   No _____

14. Do you have a relationship without any disagreements or arguments?

    Yes _____   No _____

(If you never even disagree with your partner, and think that you have a <u>perfect</u> relationship, maybe one of you is giving in too much and will someday begin to resent it.)

PERSONAL GROWTH EXERCISE - COMMON COMPLAINTS IN MARRIAGE

PURPOSE To understand some of the things which other people find annoying in their marriages, so that you can avoid them in your own life.

Following are a list of the most common complaints which are voiced consistently in marriages today. If you are married (or were married), do these sound familiar?

Women about Men

He watches too much t.v.

He won't talk

He is untidy

He won't take me anywhere

Men about Women

She talks on the phone too much

She shops too much

She "hints" instead of stating the problem

(and about women other than wives) She is a sexual teaser

If you know that even in good relationships these thing are an irritant, if not a serious problem, can you think of ways to avoid them?

CHAPTER 15

Emotional and Psychological Problems

LEARNING OBJECTIVES

1. Identify the basic concepts of abnormal behavior, and learn how the use of labels for maladaptive behavior can often distort and limit perception.

2. Understand and describe the many types of anxiety disorders, their causes and treatment.

3. Understand the major mood disorders and distinguish between the biological versus the psychological and external factors which work to cause these disorders.

CHAPTER OUTLINE

I. THE CONCEPT OF ABNORMAL BEHAVIOR
   A. Abnormal (maladaptive) Behavior: "away from the norm" implies a standard of normal behavior, however, these standards are not universally agreed upon
   B. Two Views of Abnormal Behavior:
      1. The cultural view: society is the reference, no behavior is abnormal if the majority accepts it
      2. The individual view: the same behavior may be evaluated differently when it is exhibited by two different people. The criteria would be the impairment of individual functioning or distress or harm to someone else
   C. The Use of Labels for Maladaptive Behavior
      1. Exotic labels (schizophrenia, neurotic, etc.): have become familiar to most people
      2. Labels are often given more power than they deserve
      3. Information is often limited and distorted

206 PROBLEMS THAT BLOCK EFFECTIVE BEHAVIOR

        4. Labels are neither specific nor objective, but provide a common vocabulary for communication and organization
        5. The Diagnostic and Statistical Manual for Mental Disorders (current volume DSM-III-R, third edition revised): provides a standard guide to terminology and symptoms for psychological disorders
   D. Watch Out for Student's Disease!
        1. Specific manifestation of symptoms can vary enourmously
        2. Emotional and psychological problems exist on a continuum, and degree, severity and duration must be considered
        3. Student's disease: common among medical and psychology students. They are convinced they have the disorders they are studying.

II. ANXIETY
   A. Definition: feelings of dread and apprehension, a high-energy state, physically has much in common with stress
        1. Normal anxiety has a cognitive component: worry
           a. Worry: a chain of negative and relatively uncontrollable thoughts and images of things which "might" happen
        2. Repeated short exposures to a fear-producing stimulus and very long exposures tend to extinguish the fear
        3. Exposure to real or imagined feared situations in moderate doses prolongs the fear or makes it worse. Chronic worriers put themselves in this position
        4. Borkovek: advocated controlled worrying for 30 minutes at a time
        5. Most people experience anxiety
   B. Anxiety Disorders (formerly Neuroses)
        1. An unusually high level of chronic or acute anxiety
        2. May involve maladaptive attempts to manage anxiety
        3. Generalized anxiety disorder: no identifiable stimulus (free floating anxiety), may experience a
        4. Panic attack: acute panic, symptoms may include: fainting, dizziness, sweating, shortness of breath, heart palpitations, a feeling of doom
        5. Phobic disorders: sufferers know exactly what they fear
        6. Phobia:
           a. A fear of some object or situation that is so intense it interfers with daily life
           b. May be learned through observation, social learning (imitating an adult) or indirect experience (movie, books, t.v. etc.)
           c. Phobias are learned through direct personal experience in most cases
           d. Phobias may be reinforced behavior
           e. Treatment: controlled exposure techniques
        7. Imaginal Systematic Desensitization
           a. Teach physical relaxation techniques (example: Wolpe's

progressive relaxation)
- b. An anticipatory anxiety hierarchy list (or avoidance serial-cue hierarchy) is presented beginning with the <u>least</u> threatening aspect of the feared situation and ending with direct confrontation
- c. At each step, the phobic individual imagines (or is placed in) the situation and uses the relaxation techniques in order to avoid anxiety. Once this has been achieved they move on to the next situation on their list.
- d. Works best on phobias indirectly acquired
8. Reinforced practice (or mastery treatment): when the phobic individual tackles the stimulus directly rather than mentally
    - a. Works best on phobias directly acquired
9. Treatments have a good rate of success

C. Obsessive-Compulsive Disorders
1. Definition of obsessive: unwelcome and uncontrollable thoughts
2. Definition of compulsive: acts which the individual is driven to perform (over and over again)
3. Sufferers understand they are behaving irrationally, but can't seem to stop, anxiety is high
4. Sufferers typically tend to be perfectionists, cautious, with a need to control their own lives

D. Somatoform Disorders: physical symptoms of illness or injury that have no physical organic cause, and are maladaptive ways to deal with anxiety
1. Somatization disorder:
    - a. Symptoms are chronic, extensive, onset prior to age 30
    - b. Must exhibit 12 or more physical symptoms listed in the DSM-III-R
2. Psychogenic pain disorder:
    - a. Symptom: severe and lasting pain with no organic basis
3. Hypochondriasis: obsessive preoccupation with their health and fear of disease, although most are in good health
4. Malingering: faking physical symptoms

E. Dissociative Disorders: individuals cope with anxiety by escaping from themselves
1. Amnesia: loss of memory
2. Depersonalization: loss of a sense of self
3. Multiple personality: NOT schizophrenia

F. The Causes of Anxiety Disorders:
1. Freud: anxiety is a manifestation of the struggle between the ego and the id segments of personality
2. Rogers: anxiety is caused by a discrepancy between one's true self and the standards of others
3. Widely accepted view: anxiety is a product of faulty learning:
    - a. Fears which were once specific are now generalized
    - b. Maladaptive attempts to control anxiety is also a

208 PROBLEMS THAT BLOCK EFFECTIVE BEHAVIOR

                learned behavior
- 4. Some anxiety has origins in physical causes (example: you are ill and can't study for a big exam)
- 5. Anxiety disorders are now the number one mental health problem

  G. The Treatment of Anxiety Disorders
1. A variety of methods are employed
2. Success depends on: the type of patient, duration of the problems, the form of symptoms, the diagnosis, and the relationship between the patient and therapist
3. Phobic disorders: cure rates are high
4. Somatoform disorders: poor prognosis (sympathy is a strong reinforcer to remain "sick")
5. Reduction of anxiety symptoms only: most effective treatment is medication or psychopharmacological therapy, but there are side effects and do nothing about <u>cause</u>
6. Most therapists use a combination of anti-anxiety medication and therapy

  H. Schizophrenia:
1. The label applied to a group of disorders characterized by severe personality disorientation, distortion of reality, and inability to function in daily life
2. A psychosis
3. Schizophrenics are typically withdrawn and seldom a danger to others (exception catatonic types when they are in the frenzied state, and certain paranoid types)
4. 50% of psychiatric beds are occupied by schizophrenics
5. Schizophrenics are NOT easily recognized unless in the advanced stages
6. Many "street people" are believed to be schizophrenics
7. There is a genetic susceptibility to this disorder, however environmental factors play a significant role
8. Drug therapy helps - if they can be made to take the drugs

III. DEPRESSION
  A. Definition: an overwhelming inertia, everything is too much trouble, a normal reaction to stress which is self-limiting, a disorder only when it lasts too long or is out of proportion to the stress experienced
  B. Self-help cures:
1. If they don't work, you could become more depressed
2. Depression is an adaptive state: it allows us to "let out" feelings and thoughts which are normally repressed
3. Normal depression is a temporary mood disturbance
  C. Mood Disorders: extremes of mood
1. Major depressive disorder: depression is persistent and disruptive, mood swings from normal to severe depression dominate the sufferer's whole life. Unipolar
    a. Depressive stupor: all interaction is terminated
2. Bipolar disorder: sharp swings from severe depression to

manic (formally known as manic-depressive disorder)
- a. Manic state: restless energy, grandiose schemes, uninhibited behavior, euphoric (not happy), thoughts race, seldom sleeps
- b. Women diagnosed more than men, but diagnosed men have more frequent manic episodes
- c. Onset: 25-40 years of age
- d. Suicide rate: high
- e. Chemically controllable

D. What Causes Mood Disorders?
1. Biological factors: inherited genetic disposition, born out by studies of adopted children; women diagnosed more than men but cultural factors may be a factor; the success of chemical therapy points to disruption in normal brain functioning as a cause
2. Psychological and external factors: ambitiousness, extraversion, sociability, conventionality, and high concern for the opinion of others place people at risk. Stressful life events precipitate problems
   - a. Major depression affects more urban, educated people of high occupational status than rural dwellers (suggestion: rural dwellers tend to distrust mental health professionals and do not seek help with their problems)

E. The Treatment of Mood Disorders
1. Success rate: 40-60% may expect a full recovery
2. Cognitive therapy: change the thoughts or beliefs causing or reinforcing the depression
3. Behavior therapy: change specific target behaviors by reinforcing desired behaviors and extinguishing undesired behaviors

REVIEW QUESTION

MATCHING: Match the words and phrases below with their definitions

a. abnormal behavior
b. compulsion
c. cultural view of abnormal behavior
d. somatoform disorders
e. anxiety
f. depression
g. dissociative disorders
h. individual view of abnormal behavior
i. obsession
j. worry

1. ___ Maladaptive behavior that is "away from the norm."
2. ___ The same behavior may be evaluated quite differently when it is exhibited by two different people.
3. ___ Behavior that is outside the norm for a particular society is considered to be maladaptive.
4. ___ Characterized by feeling of dread and apprehension. A high

210 PROBLEMS THAT BLOCK EFFECTIVE BEHAVIOR

          energy state.
5. ___ A chain of negative and relatively uncontrollable thoughts and images - projects you into a fear-producting situation that has not happened and may not happen.
6. ___ Unwelcome and uncontrollable thoughts.
7. ___ Acts which an individual feels driven to perform.
8. ___ Individuals cope with anxiety by escaping from themselves.
9. ___ Characterized by an overwhelming inertia, everything is just too hard.
10. ___ Characterized by physical symptoms of illness or unjury that have no physical organic cause sufficient to account for the symptoms.

PEOPLE YOU SHOULD KNOW

Borkovek
Freud
Rogers
Wolpe

FILL-IN QUESTIONS

1. The individual well-being view (Carson et al., 1988) defines _____ as any behavior that impairs individual functioning or causes distress and/or harm to others.

2. As long as they are not considered to be _____ and _____, labels are useful in the study and treatment of emotional and psychological problems.

3. One must never lose sight of the fact that emotional and psychological problems exist on a _____.

4. _____ is characterized by feelings of dread and apprehension.

5. Studies show that if one _____ the worry process, the amount of time spent worrying is reduced.

6. Almost all therapists use some form of a _____ to treat phobias.

7. _____ are acts the person feels driven to perform.

8. _____ are uncontrollable and unwelcome thoughts.

9. A generally accepted view regarding the origins of anxiety is that it is a product of _____.

10. _____ _____ involve extreme changes in mood.

EMOTIONAL AND PSYCHOLOGICAL PROBLEMS 211

11. Many people who suffer from anxiety and/or depression worry that they are "abnormal" when, in fact, their feelings are entirely within the _____.

12. The literal definition for "abnormal behavior" implies that there must be some _____ of _____ behavior; otherwise we could not know when someone's behavior is deviant.

13. The _____ consists of over 250 diagnostic codes and these are used by most professionals who treat people for emotional and psychological problems.

14. _____ is a disorder characterized by a lack of moral or ethical development (sometimes called psychopathic personality).

15. When a person is obsessed with bodily functions and has a fear of disease they are said to be suffering from _____.

16. _____ is a type of psychosis involving a systematic and organized delusion of some sort (often, but not always of persecution.

17. A severe disorder in which the personality is distorted and contact with reality is limited or nonexistant is called _____.

18. A person who is _____ manifects behavior characterized by withdrawal from reality and severe disturbances of both thought and behavior.

TRUE-FALSE QUESTIONS

T F 1. Psychological disorders consist of extremes of feelings and behaviors that are otherwise perfectly normal.

T F 2. There is a well defined standard of normal behavior which is accepted by most mental health professionals around the world.

T F 3. The standard guide to terminology and symptoms for psychological disorders is called the DSM-III-R.

T F 4. Psychosis is a severe disorder in which the personality is distorted and contact with reality is limited or nonexistant.

T F 5. At one time or another most of us have feelings or manifest symptoms that in other contexts would indicate severe emotional problems or psychological disorders.

T F 6. Student's disease is a common affliction brought about by long periods of study prior to important exams (example: during finals week).

212 PROBLEMS THAT BLOCK EFFECTIVE BEHAVIOR

T F 7. Studies in fear in humans and other animals have shown that repeated short exposures to a fear-producing stimulus and very long exposures tend to extinguish the fear response.

T F 8. A generalized anxiety disorder is characterized by a fear of some object or situation that is so intense it interferes with daily life.

T F 9. Phobias appear to be an example of learned behavior, not something a person is "born with."

T F 10. Direct exposure to a feared stimulus appears to be more effective with people who have acquired their fears indirectly (when trying to extinguish the fear).

T F 11. Persons suffering from somatization disorder claim to have many physical complaints which they do not in fact have; such as dizziness, shortness of breath, nausea, etc.

T F 12. Multiple personality disorder is a form of schizophrenia.

T F 13. Depression is a normal reaction to stress.

T F 14. It is estimated that about 40-60% of those diagnosed as having a mood disorder may expect a full recovery.

T F 15. Outside of problems with other people (difficulties with spouse, the boss, the children, and so on) anxiety and depression are the two most common problems that most psychologists, psychiatrists, and other physicians encounter.

T F 16. The continuum concept means that we must consider only the degree of unusual behavior patterns before putting labels on them; otherwise there is a risk of confusing disorders with other symptoms of known origin.

T F 17. Many forms of anxiety disorders involve maladaptive attempts to manage anxiety; the attempts are maladaptive because they end up creating more anxiety.

T F 18. To date, results of training people to "take time out for worrying" suggest that this technique increases the amount of time worriers spend with their negative thoughts and fears by about 5 percent.

T F 19. Some people become so anxious at the mere thought of talking about the feared stimulus (of their phobia) that they prefer to structure their whole lives around the phobia rather than seek treatment.

T F 20. Cognitive therapy may be described briefly as an approach to

EMOTIONAL AND PSYCHOLOGICAL PROBLEMS 213

changing behavior that focuses on changing thoughts or beliefs that may be causing (or reinforcing) the behavior.

MULTIPLE-CHOICE QUESTIONS

1. The American Psychiatric Association publishes a standard guide to terminology and symptoms for psychological disorders called the:
   a. APA-III-R
   b. DMS-III-R
   c. DSM-III-R
   d. DRS-III-R

2. A disorder in which periods of depression alternate with periods of hyperactivity and excitement.
   a. depressive disorder
   b. bi-polar disorder
   c. paranoid disorder
   d. schizophrenia

3. An irrational fear that cannot be dispelled by the intellectual knowledge that it has no basis in reality.
   a. neurosis
   b. psychosis
   c. compulsion
   d. phobia

4. A psychosis involving a systematic and organized delusion of some sort (often persecution).
   a. schizophrenia
   b. hypochondriasis
   c. conversion disorder
   d. paranoid disorder

5. Worry projects you into a fear producing situation that has not happened and may not happen; it is what part of anxiety?
   a. thinking
   b. projection
   c. normal
   d. abnormal

6. A period of acute panic that can last as long as several hours, with symptoms that include nausea, dizziness, and heart palpitations.
   a. generalized anxiety disorder
   b. phobic disorder
   c. anxiety attack
   d. psychotic episode

7. Some phobias appear to have developed because the outcome of being afraid is:
   a. frightening

b. rewarding
   c. irrational
   d. observed

8. What is one of the <u>first</u> things that most therapists do when treating phobias?
   a. ask the patient to make a hierarchial list
   b. present images of the feared object or situation
   c. expose the patient to the feared object or situation
   d. teach the patient to relax

9. What is a person classified as suffering from if they suffer physical symptoms of illness or unjury that have no physical organic cause sufficient to account for the symptoms?
   a. somatoform disorder
   b. somatization
   c. hypochondria
   d. malingering

10. Which of the following is NOT associated with schizophrenia?
    a. sometimes characterized by delusions of persecution
    b. multiple personality
    c. a common mental disorder
    d. a psychosis

11. Who believed that anxiety is a manifestation of a struggle between the ego and id segments of personality?
    a. Rogers
    b. Freud
    c. behaviorists
    d. Bandura

12. Statistics suggest that these disorders are now the number one mental health problem in this country.
    a. depressive
    b. schizophrenic
    c. anxiety
    d. somatoform

13. This disorder was originally called manic-depressive.
    a. unipolar
    b. bipolar
    c. major depressive
    d. biological depression

PEOPLE: HOW MUCH DO YOU KNOW?

Write what you can about the people listed below (as it relates to what you learned in this chapter).

<u>Borkovek</u>

<u>Freud</u>

<u>Rogers</u>

<u>Wolpe</u>

216 PROBLEMS THAT BLOCK EFFECTIVE BEHAVIOR

PERSONAL GROWTH EXERCISE - EMOTIONAL AND PSYCHOLOGICAL PROBLEMS

<u>PURPOSE</u> To show that emotional and psychological problems exist on a continuum, and that most people experience a full range of emotions at one time or another.

Comment	Always Extremely	Almost Always	Sometimes	Almost Never	Absolutely Never
	1	2 3	4	5 6	7

I am happy..................
    sad....................
    enthusiastic..........
    pensive...............
    clever................
    silly.................
    irritable.............
    energetic.............
    lethargic.............
    angry.................
    sympathetic...........
    kind..................
    unkind................
    loyal.................
    passionate............
    cold..................
    intense...............
    indecisive............
    decisive ....
    tense.................
    loose.................
    scared................
    obsessive.............
    compulsive............
    anxious...............
I worry.....................
    panic.................

If you are like most people, you will have very few checks in either the left-hand or the right-hand columns. For most of us our emotions exist on a continuum which moves between almost always and almost never. (Absolutely never and always extremely can often signal denial in an otherwise emotionally healthy person.)
It is only when we begin to notice that we <u>always</u> feel a certain way or <u>never</u> feel a certain way for long periods of time that we might begin to suspect that we have a problem (always feel something negative and never feel something positive).
If this does happen to you, you might decide to:

1. Talk things over with a friend or relative
2. See someone in the campus counseling center
3. Call your nearest mental healthcare center

218 PROBLEMS THAT BLOCK EFFECTIVE BEHAVIOR

PERSONAL GROWTH EXERCISE - WORRY

PURPOSE   To help you to understand what you worry about and to change your worry habits.

Step One   Write down 5 things that you worry about. Do this very quickly without much deliberation.

1.

2.

3.

4.

5.

Step Two   Take each of the above situations and write down the worst possible scenario. (For example: I worry about not doing well on the next test. Scenario: I flunk this whole course, and my GPA declines, I might even have to leave school altogether.)

1.

2.

3.

4.

5.

Step Three   What could you do if the worst possible scenario did occur? (For example: I would have to retake the course in order to remove the F from my transcript.)

1.

2.

3.

4.

5.

Step Four   Could you give a rational answer to the last step?

                    Yes _____   No _____

If no, then you might consider getting outside help with this problem.

Step Five   What can you do to stop what you described in step two from happening? (For example: Study hard for the exam, talk with your professor if you are having serious problems)

NOTE: Once you have dealt logically with the very worst possible thing that could happen in a given situation, that will help you to spend less time worrying about that situation.

CHAPTER

16 Getting Help: Resources for More Effective Behavior

LEARNING OBJECTIVES

1. To distinguish between the various types of therapy that are offered today.

2. To understand how your own personal support network can often prevent your problems from becoming major disturbances.

3. Describe the benefits of seeking therapy, to include what one can expect from the experience and what one should not expect.

4. Learn how to find a good therapist for you and your particular problem.

CHAPTER OUTLINE

I. SOURCES OF SUPPORT AND INFORMATION
   A. Your Support Network
      1. Family and friends:
         a. Being able to "talk it out"
         b. Receiving encouragement and support
         c. Information source
         d. Feedback about you and your behavior
   B. Other Relationship Resources
      1. People who are more objective:
         a. Rabbi, priest, minister
         b. Professor
         c. Doctor, lawyer, neighbor

222 GETTING HELP

II. PROFESSIONAL HELP
   A. Psychotherapy: the systematic use of a human relationship for therapeutic purposes. Five broad catagories:
   B. Insight Therapies: emphasis on personal history and development
      1. Psychoanalysis: stress bringing buried thoughts and wishes, which are causing internal conflict, to active memory
      2. Long lasting therapies and expensive
   C. Humanistic Therapies: focus on feelings and acceptance of self
      1. Basic assumption: people have an inherent potential for growth and self-actualization
      2. Client-centered (Rogerian or nondirective) therapy: the most well-known
         a. Establish a favorable climate
         b. Therapist shows acceptance and unconditional positive regard for the client
         c. Little or no interpretation, no judgement on the part of the therapist
         d. Therapist restates the client's words to clarify feelings
         e. Goal: clients help themselves to reduce incongruence between the true self and everyday experiences
   D. Behavior Therapies: emphasis on actions that can be observed and recorded
      1. Not much concerned with feelings, attitudes, the self, etc.
      2. Maladaptive behavior may be changed by restructuring its consequences:
         a. Positive reward for new behavior and extinction of the old behavior
         b. Change negative antecedent conditions to achieve stimulus control
         c. Contractual
   E. Cognitive Therapies: concerned with thought processes (perception, labeling, and self-talk)
      1. Cognitive-behavior therapies: seek to change behavior by changing irrational assumptions and illogical thought patterns
         a. Ellis's Rational Emotive Therapy
         b. Meichenbaum's Stress Innoculation Therapy
         c. Beck's treatment of depression:
            i. identify and explore illogical thought patterns
            ii. learn new positive, logical thought patterns
            iii. put the ideas into practice to change behavior
   F. Psychopharmacological Therapies: uses controlled prescription drugs alone or in conjuntion with other treatments
      1. Antipsychotic compounds: major tranquilizers that block a transmitter substance in the brain called dopamine, they do not cure and are used for severe psychological symptoms only

2. Antidepressant compounds: increase the concentrations of certain chemicals at locations in the brain related to depression, most common types are the tricyclics, less popular are M.A.O. inhibitors
3. Antimanic compounds: preventive chemicals, such as lithium for treatment of bi-polar disorder
4. Antianxiety compounds: most popular are the benzodiazepines which have a sedative effect

G. Who Seeks Psychological Help?
1. There is no typical client
2. Some seek help voluntarily and others are ordered to do so by the courts, or persuaded by friends or relatives
3. Voluntary clients are more likely to be female, from upper socioeconomic groups
4. Those who seek help are NOT more disturbed than other individuals

H. Does Psychological Help Help?
1. Important: the relationship between the client and the therapist
2. A client who wants and expects to receive help will benefit
3. Therapy is superior to no therapy in most cases
4. Dramatic improvements are rare

I. Shopping For a Therapist
1. Ask for recommendations
2. Check out credentials
3. Call and ask questions
4. Make an exploratory visit (without commitment)

J. What Can You Expect?
1. To be asked a number of questions
2. To take some tests for psychological assessment
3. To sit facing the therapist in comfortable surroundings
4. To talk more than to listen
5. To have what you say recorded
6. That the session will end <u>exactly</u> on time
7. To do "work" on your problems between sessions
8. To pay your bill promptly
   a. Don't be offended when asked to pay promptly

K. A Word About Cost
1. Fees range from zero to $150 and up per 50 minute session
2. Health insurance may pay all or part of the cost
3. Who benefits more, those who pay versus those who don't?
   a. Opinions differ and research is inconclusive
   b. Some studies show no difference
   c. Many studies support the no-pay argument because clients who pay more have higher expectations or because clients who are not charged directly believe in altruistic motives on the part of the therapist (the therapist is paid, however, even if not by the client)

224 GETTING HELP

      L. Saying Goodbye
1. Long-term therapy is the exception, not the rule
2. You are free to stop whenever you wish to do so
3. Leave: when you have achieved your goals, or if you feel you have made no progress
4. Do not tolerate any unethical/immoral conduct on the part of any therapist. Such cases are rare, but they do occur

III. OTHER RESOURCES
    A. Intensive Group Experiences (not group therapy): a variety of group meeting approaches that share an aim of promoting human psychological growth:
1. Encounter group: a number of people confronting one another in an intense way. The purpose is to strip away masks and pretenses and force awareness of real needs and feelings
    a. Casualties: members who are damaged by the intense group experience
    b. Success rates? A study of 117 encounter groups showed that 33% had positive changes; 18% showed negative changes (half of these were casualties); about half got very little from the experience
    c. Leadership is critical for screening members and as a safety net for participants
2. Transactional analysis (T.A.): goals are to become more accepting of themselves and others and to stop playing destructive games with one another

    B. Religion: turning to, or returning to, religion is not new
1. 1960s: Eastern religions became popular
2. 1970s: Christians were "born again"
3. Transcendental meditations, Yoga, and Zen are popular today in this country
4. Radical departures: Hare Krishnas, Moonies, Jim Jones followers, are highly controversial and outsiders believe that brainwashing and coercion are employed upon members (with some ex-members substanciating these claims)

    C. Biofeedback: an equipment-assisted method for training people to exercise control over bodily processes
Step 1: a reading is taken of the target response (for example: the heartrate)
Step 2: this is electronically converted to a visual signal or a sound
Step 3: the signal is transmitted (fed back) to the subject
These steps are the basis for training the subject to influence the response in a desired fashion (for example: tension headaches may be controlled, blood pressure may be reduced)

RESOURCES FOR MORE EFFECTIVE BEHAVIOR 225

    D. Hypnosis: a hypnotic trance enables the therapist to gain access to hidden feelings and memories
        1. Post-hypnotic suggestion: an idea about how an individual will behave in the future is "planted" through verbal suggestion while the person is in a trance
        2. Success rate: 10% cannot achieve a trance at all and a large percentage of the population cannot achieve a deep trance
        3. Be sure to consult a trained professional

IV. PUTTING IT ALL TOGETHER

    ONE: Study yourself. If you want to change, make a plan

    TWO: Work on accepting yourself as a valuable human being

    THREE: Become involved with other people

    FOUR: Remember that you have the ability to control your own life

REVIEW QUESTIONS

MATCHING: Match the words and phrases below with the definitions

a. casualties
b. client-centered therapy
c. cognitive-behavior therapy
d. effective behavior
e. humanistic therapy
f. insight therapy
g. psychopharmacological therapy
h. Alzheimer's disease
i. behavior therapy
j. biofeedback

1. __f__ The premise that we must have understanding of our basic motivations and how we came to be the way we are if we are to experience relief from symptoms or change something about ourselves. Considerable emphasis is placed on personal history and development.
2. __e__ The focus is on feelings, and share a belief that people have an inherent potential for growth and self-actualization and this can be released through the exploration of feelings and a greater acceptance of self.
3. __b__ Rogerian therapy which emphasizes the critical importance of the therapist's role in establishing a favorable climate for the client's exploration of true thoughts and feelings.
4. __i__ Emphasis is placed on behaviors that can be observed and recorded, and practitioners share a belief that maladaptive behavior may be changed directly by restructuring its consequences.

226 GETTING HELP

5. _C_ Concerned with thought processes, including how we perceive things, how we label things, and how we talk to ourselves, and are involved with helping people to change their behavior by changing irrational assumptions and illogical thinking patterns that cause the behavior.
6. _g_ Treats psychological symptoms partially or entirely by means of controlled prescription drugs.
7. _h_ A disorder resulting from deterioration of the brain. Symptoms include decreased mental alertness and adaptability, increased self-centeredness and periods of confusion and agitation.
8. _a_ Individuals who experience severely negative effects after a group encounter session.
9. _j_ An equipment-assisted method for training people to be able to exercise some control over such bodily processes as blood pressure, heart rate, muscle contraction, and temperature.
10. _d_ Flexible, controlled, and productive behavior that allows us to feel good about ourselves and others as we move toward understanding ourselves and achieving realistic personal goals and good relationships.

PEOPLE YOU SHOULD KNOW

Berne
Knapp
Jim Jones
Lieberman, Yalom and Miles
Rogers
Beck
Alzheimer

FILL-IN QUESTIONS

1. _psycho analytic & insight_ therapies place considerable emphasis on personal history and development.

2. Humanistic approaches focus on _feelings_ and a greater acceptance of _self_.

3. Cognitive therapists are concerned with the _thought process_.

4. _psychopharmacological_ therapy treats psychological symptoms partially or entirely by means of controlled prescription drugs.

5. Major tranquilizers block a transmitter substance in the brain called _dopamine_.

6. _benzodiazepines_, such as librium and valium, are used to treat anxiety.

7. A disease which might be mistaken for natural changes due to the

aging process is _Alzheimers_.

8. Clients who pay more for psychological services tend to claim _lower_ success rates for the help received.

9. The more common form of intensive group experience is the _encounter group_.

10. _Biofeedback_ is an equipment-assisted method for training people to be able to exercise some control over bodily processes.

11. _Effective behavior_ has been defined as flexible, controlled, and productive behavior that allows us to feel good about ourselves and others as we move toward understanding ourselves and achieving realistic personal goals and good relationships.

12. The first line of defense for most of us when we find that we need some help is _family / friends_

13. Strupp defined _psychotherapy_ as the systematic use of a human relationship for therapeutic purposes.

14. The most traditional form of insight therapy with us today is _psychoanalysis_ and its various modifications.

15. Carl Rogers believed that reducing the _incongruence_ between the true self and everyday experience (which usually includes hiding the true self) is what is required for a healthy personality, good personal relationships, and the elimination of such maladaptive experiences as anxiety.

16. Most behavior therapists concentrate on the _positive reinforcement_ of desired new beahviors along with extinction of undesired old behavior.

TRUE-FALSE QUESTIONS

(T) F 1. For most of us, the first line of defense when we need some help is family and/or friends and this is not a bad place to start.

(T) F 2. Client-centered therapists rely upon restatement; he or she repeats in a different way and without any judgements what the client seems to be saying.

(T) F 3. Practitioners of behavioral therapies believe that maladaptive behavior may be changed directly by restructuring its consequences.

T (F) 4. Cognitive-behavioralist, Beck, treats people who are suffering from depression by administering a post-hypnotic suggestion.

(T) F 5. Lithium is the chemical treatment of choice for bi-polar disorder.

(T) F 6. An antipsychotic, like thorazine, mellaril or haldol, would be used to treat schizophrenia.

T (F) 7. A psychologist must have a medical degree in order to practice in some states.

(T) F 8. Of primary importance to the success of therapy is the relationship between the client and the therapist, and not the method of therapy used.

T (F) 9. If you do choose to seek the help of a therapist, you will be put at ease during therapy by relaxing on a couch in the office while you answer questions about your problem.

(T) F 10. During all types of therapy you will do more talking than the therapist/counselor.

(T) F 11. Many therapists will give their clients "homework" to be completed between sessions.

(T) F 12. Many people seem to think that there is something low and money-grubbing about asking the clients of psychological services to pay their bills because they have enough problems without adding financial worries to them.

T (F) 13. There is conclusive evidence that people who do not have to pay directly for mental health services appear to consider the help they receive to be more worthwhile than those who have to pay for services.

T (F) 14. The term intensive group experience is another way of saying group therapy.

T (F) 15. Levine (1984) stated that the ultimate use of religious resources for personal help lies in what he called radical departures, by which he meant departing an established life pattern to take up residence and allegience to a radical religious group, such as the Hare Krishnas, the "Moonies," or Jim Jones followers.

MULTIPLE-CHOICE QUESTIONS

1. The most traditional form of insight therapies which emphasizes the importance of bringing buried thoughts and wishes that are causing internal conflict to active memory.

a. hypnosis
b. psychoanalysis ✓
c. cognitive
d. client-centered

2. In this type of therapy, the therapist repeats in different words what is told to him or her by the client.
   a. humanistic
   b. psychoanalysis
   c. Rogerian ✓
   d. cognitive

3. What kind of therapy concentrates on positive reinforcement of desired actions along with the extinction of undesired actions?
   a. client-centered
   b. behavioral ✓
   c. cognitive
   d. humanistic

4. Ellis's rational emotive therapy and Meichenbaum's stress innoculation therapy are methods of _____ therapy.
   a. behavioral
   b. cognitive
   c. cognitive-behavioral ✓
   d. humanistic

5. Which of the following would NOT be a basic step in Beck's treatment of depression?
   a. identify and explore illogical thought processes
   b. learn logical positive thought processes
   c. use new techniques to change behavior
   d. learn relaxation techniques ✓

6. The major tranquilizers which block a transmitter substance in the brain called dopamine belong to which catagory of drug compounds?
   a. antipsychotic ✓
   b. antidepressant
   c. antimanic
   d. antianxiety

7. What is the disorder whose symptoms include decreased mental alertness and adaptability, increased self-centeredness, low tolerance for change, periods of confusion and agitation, and impaired memory and judgement?
   a. schizophrenia
   b. bi-polar disorder
   c. Alzheimer's disease ✓
   d. somatoform disorder

8. What is the most critical aspect of therapy for the treatment to be considered sucessful?

230 GETTING HELP

    a. the relationship between the client and the therapist
    b. the type of therapy used
    c. the experience of the therapist
    d. the setting for the sessions (comfortable)

9. Which of the following is NOT recommended when shopping for a therapist?
    a. ask for recommendations
    b. check the yellow pages
    c. make an exploratory visit
    d. check credentials

10. Some people are hurt, surprised, and even angry to discover that their session is ended precisely on time, no matter what is happening. These people are more likely to be visiting which kind of therapist?
    a. behavioral
    b. cognitive
    c. Rogerian
    d. any of the above

11. Which type of therapy treats psychological symptoms by means of controlled prescription drugs?
    a. psychotherapy
    b. hypnosis
    c. psychopharmacological
    d. pharmacological

12. Which group of drugs is used to treat the following symptoms: extreme agitation, hallucinations, aggressive behavior, and delusions?
    a. antidepressant
    b. antimanic
    c. antianxiety
    d. antipsychotic

13. Which group of drugs is used to treat the following symptoms: manic behavior, depression that alternates with mania?
    a. antidepressant
    b. antimanic
    c. antianxiety
    d. antipsychotic

14. Which group of drugs is used to treat the following symptoms: chronic insomnia, tension?
    a. antidepressant
    b. antimanic
    c. antianxiety
    d. antipsychotic

15. Which of the following group of drugs has serious side effects?
    a. antidepressant
    b. antianxiety
    c. antipsychotic
    (d.) all have serious and dangerous side effects

PEOPLE: HOW MUCH DO YOU KNOW?

Write what you can about the people listed below (as it relates to what you learned in this chapter).

Berne

Knapp

Jim Jones

Lieberman, Yalom and Miles

Rogers

232 GETTING HELP

Beck

Alzheimer

PERSONAL GROWTH EXERCISE - WHAT TYPE OF THERAPY?

PURPOSE To understand the application of various types of therapy to various problems which you, your relatives or friends, might come into contact with at some time during your lifetime.

Your text lists many different types of therapy (insight, humanistic, behavior, cognitive psychopharmacological, intensive group experiences, biofeedback, hypnosis, psychodynamic). Some of these methods might be more successful with certain disorders or problems than others. If you, or a friend/relative, were suffering from the following problems what type of therapy would you recommend, and why?

1. marital:

2. sexual:

3. interpersonal at work/school:

4. interpersonal at home/with relatives:

5. anxiety:

6. phobia:

7. communication:

8. schizophrenia:

9. drug abuse:

10. alcoholism:

11. eating disorder

12. low self-esteem

13. Alzheimer's disease

14. paranoia:

15. shyness:

16. obsessive disorder:

17. compulsive disorder:

18. antisocial personality disorder:

19. adjustment disorder:

20. compulsive lying:

Do you feel that there are any of these problems which do not need any professional help, including that from self-help books or tapes?

                Yes _____   No _____

If yes, which problems are these and how would you handle them?

If no, which problems do you think could possibly be helped by books or tapes?

Which problems would you consider to need professional help as soon as possible?

Do you know anyone suffering from one of the above problems?

PERSONAL GROWTH EXERCISE - YOUR OWN PROBLEMS

<u>PURPOSE</u> To identify your own methods for dealing with problems as they occur in your life.

How do you deal with your problems when they occur?

You have a problem with:

    a. school:

    b. close relationship:

    c. family:

    d. friends:

    e. your boss:

    f. your teacher:

    g. finances:

    h. sex:

Have you ever bought a self-help book or tape to help you solve a problem?

                Yes _____   No _____

If yes, did you find the information helpful?

                Yes _____   No _____

If no, would you consider buying such a book or tape in the future for a different problem?

                Yes _____   No _____

236 GETTING HELP

Would you ever visit a therapist if a problem became too difficult for you to deal with alone?

Yes _____   No _____

What type of therapist do you think you could relate to?

What would you expect from a therapist?

Your text describes the differences in the outcome of treatment when people pay for treatment versus when they do not pay for treatment. Do you think that everyone should have to pay for mental healthcare services? Why, or why not?

ANSWERS TO CHAPTER 1

MATCHING

1. c 2. a 3. i 4. d 5. j
6. b 7. f 8. h 9. e 10. g

FILL-IN

1. effective behavior
2. realistically
3. effective behavior
4. constraints
5. norms
6. adjustment
7. choice
8. control
9. scientific method
10. logic
11. theories
12. conservatism
13. psychology

TRUE-FALSE

1. F   6. T   11. T
2. F   7. T   12. T
3. T   8. T   13. F
4. T   9. T   14. F
5. F   10. F 15. T

MULTIPLE-CHOICE

1. d   6. a   11. c
2. a   7. b   12. b
3. d   8. d   13. a
4. b   9. c   14. c
5. c   10. a 15. a

ANSWERS TO CHAPTER 2

MATCHING

1. b   2. c   3. g   4. h   5. i
6. a   7. d   8. f   9. e   10. j

FILL-IN

1. psychology
2. personal; environmental
3. interaction
4. attitude
5. indirect
6. physical
7. density; crowded
8. social
9. norms
10. social
11. expectations
12. beliefs
13. anonymity
14. indifference

TRUE-FALSE

1. T   8. F   15. F
2. T   9. T   16. F
3. F   10. T   17. F
4. T   11. F   18. F
5. T   12. T   19. T
6. T   13. F   20. T
7. F   14. F

MULTIPLE-CHOICE

1. c   6. c   11. d
2. b   7. d   12. d
3. d   8. b
4. b   9. c
5. a   10. a

ANSWERS TO CHAPTER 3

MATCHING

1. b　　2. f　　3. a　　4. h　　5. j
6. i　　7. e　　8. d　　9. g　　10. c

FILL-IN

1. classical
2. reinforcers
3. negative
4. punishment
5. ignoring
6. continuous; intermittent
7. moral
8. dilemmas
9. values
10. society; individual

TRUE-FALSE

1. T　　8. F　　15. F
2. F　　9. F　　16. T
3. F　　10. T　　17. T
4. T　　11. T　　18. F
5. T　　12. T　　19. F
6. T　　13. T　　20. T
7. F　　14. T

MULTIPLE-CHOICE

1. c　　6. d
2. a　　7. c
3. b　　8. b
4. d　　9. d
5. b　　10. d

ANSWERS TO CHAPTER 4

MATCHING

1. a 2. b 3. e 4. d 5. f
6. c 7. g 8. h 9. i 10. j

FILL-IN

1. personality
2. individuality
3. locus of control
4. support
5. id; ego; superego
6. displacement
7. slip
8. adolescence
9. identity crisis
10. antecedents
11. biological
12. learned
13. personality
14. antisocial
15. prevent; change

TRUE-FALSE

1. T
2. F
3. T
4. T
5. T
6. F
7. F
8. T
9. F
10. T
11. T
12. T
13. T
14. T
15. F

MULTIPLE-CHOICE

1. d
2. c
3. a
4. b
5. c
6. a
7. c
8. a
9. c
10. b

ANSWERS TO CHAPTER 5

MATCHING

1. b   2. h   3. i   4. d   5. f
6. j   7. c   8. a   9. e   10. g

FILL-IN

1. self
2. empathy
3. positive
4. peers and friends
5. stereotype
6. transsexualism
7. sex
8. androgeny
9. consciousness; description
10. self-esteem

TRUE-FALSE

1. F   6. T   11. T   16. T
2. T   7. T   12. T   17. F
3. T   8. F   13. F   18. T
4. T   9. F   14. T   19. F
5. F   10. T   15. T   20. F

MULTIPLE-CHOICE

1. c   6. b
2. a   7. b
3. d / B   8. d
4. c   9. c
5. a   10. d

ANSWERS TO CHAPTER 6

MATCHING

1. a   2. h   3. i   4. j   5. e
6. g   7. f   8. c   9. d   10. b

FILL-IN

1. attachment
2. critical period
3. peers; peer groups
4. adolescence
5. buffer
6. support groups
7. 15 and 35
8. involving strategies
9. social interaction
10. proximity, similarity, and reciprocity
11. early

TRUE-FALSE

1. F   9. T   17. T
2. T   10. T
3. T   11. F
4. F   12. F
5. F   13. T
6. T   14. T
7. F   15. F
8. T   16. F

MULTIPLE-CHOICE

1. b   8. d   15. b
2. d   9. c   16. a
3. a   10. d   17. d
4. c   11. b   18. c
5. a   12. a   19. c
6. a   13. a   20. a
7. b   14. c   21. b

ANSWERS TO SELF TEST QUESTIONS   243

ANSWERS TO CHAPTER 7

MATCHING

1. b   2. c   3. d   4. e   5. i
6. f   7. h   8. j   9. a   10. g

FILL-IN

1. sex drive
2. androgens; testosterone
3. estrogens; ovaries
4. fellatio; cunnilingus
5. refractory period
6. excitement; plateau; orgasmic; resolution
7. birth control pill
8. swinging
9. 27,000; every day
10. A.I.D.S.

TRUE-FALSE

1. F   6. T   11. T   16. T
2. F   7. F   12. F   17. T
3. T   8. T   13. T   18. F
4. F   9. F   14. F   19. T
5. T   10. F   15. T   20. F

MULTIPLE-CHOICE

1. d   8. c   15. c
2. c   9. a   16. d
3. d   10. d   17. d
4. b   11. a   18. c
5. b   12. a   19. a
6. d   13. b   20. b
7. b   14. a

ANSWERS TO CHAPTER 8

MATCHING

1. a   2. g   3. e   4. i   5. j
6. c   7. b   8. f   9. h   10. d

FILL-IN

1. behavioral
2. humanistic
3. triangle theory of love
4. romantic by nature
5. perfection
6. 23; 24; 26
7. love
8. personal freedom
9. trial marriage
10. life style adjustment
11. prenuptual agreement
12. about money

TRUE-FALSE

1. F   6. F   11. T   16. F
2. T   7. T   12. F   17. F
3. F   8. F   13. T   18. F
4. T   9. T   14. T
5. T   10. F   15. T

MULTIPLE-CHOICE

1. d   8. a   15. d   22. c
2. a   9. c   16. b
3. b   10. d   17. b
4. c   11. b   18. a
5. d   12. a   19. d
6. b   13. c   20. c
7. c   14. c   21. b

ANSWERS TO CHAPTER 9

MATCHING

1. j 2. g 3. c 4. d 5. e
6. a 7. h 8. i 9. b 10. f

FILL-IN

1. studying
2. distributed study time
3. outline answer
4. plan ahead
5. an interest inventory
6. skills; ability
7. west; southwest; Florida
8. <u>The Occupational Outlook Handbook</u> (Bureau of Labor Statistics)
9. unfair discrimination
10. trying it
11. do well at the interview

TRUE-FALSE

1. T   6. F   11. F   16. F
2. F   7. F   12. T   17. T
3. T   8. F   13. T   18. F
4. T   9. F   14. F   19. T
5. T   10. T   15. T

MULTIPLE-CHOICE

1. b   7. d   13. a
2. c   8. a   14. b
3. a   9. b   15. d
4. d   10. c   16. c
5. c   11. d
6. d   12. d

ANSWERS TO SELF TEST QUESTIONS

ANSWERS TO CHAPTER 10

MATCHING

1. d	2. c	3. f	4. j	5. e
6. h	7. i	8. g	9. a	10. b

FILL-IN

1. decoding
2. one-way communication
3. effective
4. surplus meaning and relationship threats
5. noise
6. displaced aggression
7. the telephone
8. loaded words
9. men; women
10. salience
11. nonverbal communication
12. evaluations
13. pseudoquestions
14. fogging
15. hearing
16. active listening

TRUE-FALSE

1. T	7. F	13. T
2. T	8. T	14. T
3. T	9. T	15. F
4. F	10. T	16. F
5. T	11. T	17. F
6. F	12. F	18. T

MULTIPLE-CHOICE

1. d	7. d	13. b	19. c
2. b	8. b	14. a	20. b
3. c	9. a	15. b	21. d
4. a	10. d	16. a	22. b
5. c	11. a	17. a	23. a
6. a	12. d	18. a	24. a

ANSWERS TO CHAPTER 11

MATCHING

1. c 2. g 3. h 4. f 5. d
6. a 7. b 8. j 9. e 10. i

FILL-IN

1. decision
2. problem
3. psychological
4. clear, measurable, and attainable
5. constraints
6. maximizing; satisficing
7. cognitive limits
8. regret
9. balance sheet
10. decision
11. maximizing
12. set the criteria
13. uncertainty
14. information overload
15. cognitive limits
16. decision aids; decision tree
17. hot cognitions

TRUE-FALSE

1. T   7. T   13. T   19. F
2. T   8. F   14. T   20. T
3. F   9. F   15. F
4. T   10. F 16. T
5. T   11. T 17. T
6. F   12. T 18. T

MULTIPLE-CHOICE

1. b   6. b   11. c
2. c   7. c
3. d   8. a
4. a   9. d
5. c   10. b

ANSWERS TO CHAPTER 12

MATCHING

1. a   2. b   3. c   4. d   5. j
6. h   7. e   8. f   9. i   10. g

FILL-IN

1. relationship
2. stressors
3. frustration
4. General Adaptation Syndrome
5. displacement
6. energy
7. eustress
8. unexpected
9. time
10. assertive
11. changes
12. repression
13. oversimplification

TRUE-FALSE

1. T   6. F   11. T   16. F
2. F   7. F   12. T   17. T
3. T   8. F   13. F   18. T
4. T   9. T   14. F
5. T   10. T   15. T

MULTIPLE-CHOICE

1. b   7. d   13. b   19. d
2. c   8. c   14. a   20. d
3. d   9. b   15. c   21. a
4. c   10. c   16. d   22. c
5. b   11. d   17. b   23. b
6. a   12. d   18. c   24. b

ANSWERS TO SELF TEST QUESTIONS   249

ANSWERS TO CHAPTER 13

MATCHING

1. a   2. h   3. e   4. i   5. b
6. f   7. g   8. j   9. c   10. d

FILL-IN

1. addiction
2. nicotine
3. blood alcohol concentration
4. 60
5. Korsakoff's psychosis
6. antabuse
7. barbituates
8. marijuana
9. "set point"
10. Basal Metabolic Rate (BMR)
11. mouth and throat
12. caffeine
13. behavioral
14. drug
15. cocaine
16. marijuana
17. BMR
18. anorexia nervosa

TRUE-FALSE

1. T   6. F   11. T   16. T
2. T   7. T   12. F   17. T
3. T   8. F   13. F   18. T
4. T   9. F   14. T   19. F
5. F   10. T   15. F   20. T

MULTIPLE-CHOICE

1. d   6. b   11. d   16. c
2. d   7. b   12. b
3. a   8. d   13. c
4. c   9. c   14. d
5. c   10. a   15. b

ANSWERS TO SELF TEST QUESTIONS

ANSWERS TO CHAPTER 14

MATCHING

1. f
2. e
3. h
4. j
5. i
6. d
7. g
8. c
9. b
10. a

FILL-IN

1. more
2. improving social skills
3. situational
4. norms
5. competance
6. more intelligent
7. jealousy
8. one-sided; mutual
9. men; women
10. private
11. public
12. social
13. shy
14. emotional
15. expectations
16. competence
17. "not willing"
18. more difficult than ever
19. jealousy, hostility and lack of trust
20. climate

TRUE-FALSE

1. F
2. T
3. T
4. F
5. T
6. T
7. F
8. F
9. T
10. T
11. F
12. T
13. T
14. F

MULTIPLE-CHOICE

1. c
2. d
3. b
4. c
5. a
6. b
7. c
8. d
9. d
10. d
11. c
12. a
13. b
14. c
15. d

ANSWERS TO CHAPTER 15

MATCHING

1. a   2. h   3. c   4. e   5. j
6. i   7. b   8. g   9. f   10. d

FILL-IN

1. abnormal behavior
2. specific; objective
3. continuum
4. anxiety
5. isolate
6. controlled exposure technique
7. compulsions
8. obsessions
9. faulty learning
10. mood disorders
11. normal range
12. standard; normal
13. DSM-III-R
14. antisocial personality
15. hypochondriasis
16. paranoid disorder
17. psychosis
18. schizophrenia

TRUE-FALSE

1. T   6. F   11. F   16. F
2. F   7. T   12. F   17. T
3. T   8. F   13. T   18. F
4. T   9. T   14. T   19. T
5. T   10. F   15. T   20. T

MULTIPLE-CHOICE

1. c   6. c   11. b
2. b   7. b   12. c
3. d   8. d   13. b
4. d   9. a
5. a   10. b

ANSWERS TO CHAPTER 16

MATCHING

1. f   2. e   3. b   4. i   5. c
6. g   7. h   8. a   9. j   10. d

FILL-IN

1. insight
2. feelings; self
3. thought processes
4. psychopharmacological
5. dopamine
6. benzodiazepines
7. Alzheimer's disease
8. lower
9. encounter group
10. biofeedback
11. effective behavior
12. family/friends
13. psychotherapy
14. psychoanalysis
15. incongruence
16. positive reinforcement

TRUE-FALSE

1. T   6. T   11. T
2. T   7. F   12. T
3. T   8. T   13. F
4. F   9. F   14. F
5. T   10. T   15. F

MULTIPLE-CHOICE

1. b   6. a   11. c
2. c   7. c   12. d
3. b   8. a   13. b
4. c   9. b   14. c
5. d   10. d   15. d